"Get ready to dig in—deep—to *Rich Soil* and discover the eight strategies for maximizing your impact as a leader. Dan Martin reveals time-tested secrets of being more strategic, effective, and efficient. Read this book and you'll have the tools for helping any business or organization more effectively fulfill its mission. It's poignant, practical, and grounded. Don't miss out on this transformative message."

—Les Parrott
No. 1 *New York Times* best-selling author of *You're Stronger Than You Think*

"*Rich Soil* offers solid, actionable advice tying a leader's heart to an organization's success. As a trustee for Seattle Pacific University, I've seen Dan Martin effectively use many of these leadership principles to strengthen SPU into a leading Christian university. These principles apply to leaders at all levels—from a family to a global institution."

—Richard Stearns
President of World Vision U.S.
Author of *Unfinished* and *The Hole in Our Gospel*

"I often say, 'I used to be afraid of failing at something that really mattered to me, but now I'm more afraid of succeeding at things that don't matter.' In this book, Dan Martin illustrates concepts and tools that will enable leaders and managers to define, position, and advance 'what matters' for success."

—Bob Goff
New York Times best-selling author of *Love Does*

RICH SOIL

RICH SOIL

TRANSFORMING YOUR ORGANIZATION'S LANDSCAPE FOR MAXIMUM EFFECTIVENESS

DANIEL J. MARTIN

BEACON HILL PRESS
OF KANSAS CITY

ISBN 978-0-8341-3245-0

Printed in the
United States of America

Cover Design: Jared Dunn
Interior Design: Sharon Page

Library of Congress Cataloging-in-Publication Data
Martin, Daniel J.
  Rich soil : transforming your organization's landscape for maximum effectiveness / Daniel J. Martin.
    pages cm
  Includes bibliographical references and index.
  ISBN 978-0-8341-3245-0 (pbk. : alk. paper)
  1. Organizational effectiveness. 2. Organizational change. 3. Strategic planning.
4. Success in business. I. Title.
  HD58.9.M3777 2014
  658.4'06—dc23

                                                                          2014018987

10 9 8 7 6 5 4 3 2 1

CONTENTS

INTRODUCTION

Throughout the history of American business, the organizational landscape has become filled with built-from-scratch success stories —McDonald's, Apple, Microsoft, Starbucks, Twitter, Facebook, Amazon.com—the list goes on and on. This book tells the story of yet another—Joe & Chow's.

Joe & Chow's, a quickly growing national coffeehouse chain, was founded when a young professional named Will lost his job due to the economic downturn. His wife, Maddie, encouraged him to pursue his dream by beginning small. With a unique vision, a focused mission, a well-resourced equity partner, and a tremendous amount of hard work, Will opened a single coffeehouse. From there, Joe & Chow's experienced explosive growth—and the rest is history.

Oh, wait. You haven't heard of Joe & Chow's? That's because this is a *story* about a great American business. Although it portrays a fictional company, this book is built on timeless business principles. The story is written in a clear, easy-to-read style that will allow you to immerse yourself in the strategies it presents. No matter what type of business or organization you're in, Will's story will easily translate to your own leadership and management experiences. Whether you're a manager, CEO, executive director, or just beginning your career, this book illustrates practical leadership and management insights that will aid you in establishing a foundation for organizational success.

The core of the story is a framework of eight elements that are critical for organizational success. These elements form a road map for any business seeking to improve its performance and more effectively fulfill its mission. To see the eight elements in action, pay special attention to the "rich soil" tips numbered and located throughout the narrative and marked with the symbol ♠. End-of-chapter sections keyed to the tip numbers in a particular chapter discuss the elements the chapter is illustrating. Once you've finished reading the story, see the appendix for prompts that will aid you in applying the elements to your own organizational context.

In today's business world, the external environment is more complex than ever. The pace of change is unprecedented, new competitors emerge daily, and the economy has shifted dramatically. For those reasons, there has never been a better time to improve your organization's strategy, effectiveness, and efficiency. Will's story and resulting observations illustrate ways to do just that.

This book does not contain all the answers, but it does contain insights that will encourage and prepare you for your current and future leadership opportunities. What's more, it will serve as a catalyst for improving your organization's performance.

JACK

The office was silent as I settled in for a night of work. I began paging through my flip charts in an attempt to identify each aspect of the business that needed attention. I tried to detail some action steps, but it all seemed so disjointed. As I struggled to piece my thoughts together, I felt a knot of anxiety forming in my stomach. I knew that unless my team understood what made our business distinct, any plan would break down quickly.

I stopped for a moment and reflected on how Joe & Chow's had changed from the time I led it independently. It was definitely a different company now, but I struggled to determine where to go from here. Some said we simply needed to take action in key problem areas. But I was convinced that even if I took action, the bigger questions would remain: Where was Joe & Chow's going? Why did we exist?

As the night went on and my frustration began to wear on me, my thoughts drifted back to the early days of Joe & Chow's. I missed George. I could have met him for lunch or a cup of coffee and told him what I was facing, and he would have cut through all the haze and given me a piece of solid wisdom—wisdom that would provide me with a framework for moving forward.

Then the memory struck me. When I first talked with George about my ideas for Joe & Chow's, he had given me a document filled with miscellaneous thoughts and ideas about starting a business. I spun around to search my file drawer. Maybe reviewing his notes would help me recapture the inspiration for Joe & Chow's, as well as formulate a plan.

After looking through my files with no luck, I glanced at the clock to see that it was just past midnight. I took a break from searching for the notes, leaned back, and closed my eyes. I tried to imagine what George would do in this situation. What questions would he ask? What advice would he have given me for my meeting with Richard?

Suddenly, a crash jolted me awake (I had dozed off). I had thought I was the only one in the building. As I moved quietly to the door, I peered around the corner and saw a maintenance man sweeping up what appeared to be glass from the light fixture.

I stepped into the hall. "Hello?"

An old, weathered man looked up from behind the cart and gave me a gentle smile. "Oh, I didn't know anyone was here. I was working on this fixture when it fell. I'll get this cleaned up and be out of your way."

"It's no problem. I was in my office and wanted to come see what happened. I'm Will." I extended my hand.

"I'm Jack," he smiled. "Whatever you're working on must be important if you're going at it this late."

"I guess you could say my lifelong dream depends on it. So yeah, it's important. If you can tell me how to turn this business around, let me know, okay?" I laughed.

He looked at me intently. "I may not have the answer, but I can listen. Have a seat. Looks like you've been working hard." He motioned to one of the chairs in the lobby.

After a moment's hesitation, I sat down across from him. *What's there to lose?* I thought. At least it was an opportunity to talk things out.

For the next two hours I told Jack about how I founded the business, the sale to Charter/Keel, purchasing it back with Richard as my partner, and the challenges I had encountered with my attempts to turn the business around. All the while, Jack just listened.

"So," I finally concluded, "I had dinner with Richard tonight and promised him a plan by Wednesday. On top of that, I said we would turn a profit within three months. There, that's the story. Do you have any advice?" I smiled wryly. Even though I didn't expect answers from Jack, I found that recounting the story made me feel better.

Jack was silent for a moment, then looked me in the eye. "I don't know if I have any advice for you," he began. "But I do want to tell you a story that has some uncanny similarities."

He leaned forward in his seat. "There was man who grew up in the suburbs—he played sports, earned high marks in school, and, after finishing high school, did as was expected of him—he went off to college and chose a sensible major. After graduating with an accounting degree, he secured a position as an auditor at a prestigious public accounting firm. He passed his CPA exam on his first try, then began, by all appearances, an ideal career that would provide a stable life.

"But ever since he was a little boy, he had loved spending summers at his grandparents' farm. He loved getting his hands dirty, watching the cycles of growth in the fields, and seeing the difference the farm made in the lives of all those who benefited from it.

"Despite this passion, he played it safe and continued in his corporate career. He was quite successful: he became a partner at his firm before he was thirty, he married a beautiful woman, and soon he and she were expecting their first child. However, deep inside, he wasn't truly happy with his career. Finally, he confessed to his wife his desire to become a farmer. She was supportive, and within a year, he had purchased a farm near where his grandparents lived.

"The first spring at the farm, he went out to sow seeds. As he drove a tractor through the fields, some seeds fell along the path. Because the soil was so hard, the seeds failed to take root. Some remained there, while others were eaten by birds.

"Later, other seeds fell in soil that was filled with rocks. Although some seeds found crevices to grow in, the land was so rocky that the roots couldn't grow deep. The sun scorched the plants, and they withered and died. Still other seeds fell among some weeds. The weeds lived in healthy soil, but as the seeds grew, the weeds choked out the healthy plants."

"However, some of the seeds fell in good soil. Because of this, the roots took hold in rich, nutritious earth and yielded a tremendous crop, a hundred times more than was sown."

Suddenly Jack stopped, looked at me, and said, "If you listen, you will hear."

GEORGE DOES IT AGAIN

I woke up to the sound of my cell phone ringing. As I clumsily grasped for it, I saw Maddie's name on the display.

"Hello?"

"Are you okay?" Her voice was filled with concern. "Did you come home at all last night?"

I blinked. I had fallen asleep at the office again. I squinted at the clock—5:00 a.m. Slowly, I remembered my conversation with Jack. I got up from my desk and walked out to the hall to see if he was still around. "Yeah, I'm doing okay. I fell asleep at my desk. I'm going to come home to eat and get ready for the day."

"Okay. I love you," she replied.

Jack wasn't in the hall. I checked the lower two floors and didn't find him there either. *I didn't dream it all, did I?* I asked myself in disbelief. As I walked back to my office, I wondered why he had thought the story of an accountant turned farmer would mean anything to me.

When I went back to my office to gather my things, I saw the files I had been rifling through the night before. On top of the files lay a few pieces of paper covered with handwriting. As I walked closer, I was surprised to find that they were George's notes. How in the world had they gotten there? And why hadn't I seen them there the night before? Bewildered, I sat down and began reading.

Considerations as You Begin Joe & Chow's

1. Have a firm understanding of why you are in business. What is the mission of Joe & Chow's? When you answer that question, you will have uncovered your **reason** for existence! Your reason must shape everything the organization does—conversations, daily operations, policies, and your operational and strategic planning.

2. What is the vision for Joe & Chow's? Where will the company be in five to ten years? You must **imagine** the future, then take substantive steps to achieve it! The mission will inform why and how you do business; the vision will determine where and what the business will be. Though you as the leader are responsible for developing that vision, it is best if it is developed with board members, employees, and others who will have a role in fulfilling it.

3. Once the planning process is completed and the mission and vision are defined, you must make sure the entire organization is on the same page. The mission and vision must be articulated with **clarity**.

4. Beyond clarity, you must have **harmony** within your team at every level. Think of it as a band. You need professionals in each instrument section, but to create music and reach a high standard of performance, they must complement each other and work together.

5. As you flesh out how the team will implement the mission and vision, be sure to develop **strategic** thoughts for progressing toward your vision. At the same time, your strategy should reinforce and strengthen the culture you will create at Joe & Chow's.

6. In order for Joe & Chow's to be efficient and effective, the strategy must be **operational**. The strategy shouldn't be so

esoteric that it is unable to drive the organization to its goals; it must frame daily decisions and progress. The strategy will determine the direction and destination, as well as maintain your organization's purpose and identity, but first, it must be operationalized.

7. Many companies make good strategic and operational plans but ultimately fail to act on them. For Joe & Chow's to be successful, you must **implement** your plan. The plan won't do you any good if you stop at creating it. Creating plans can be enjoyable and energizing, but implementing plans can be tedious and frustrating, since it is the point at which you will encounter the most resistance to change.

8. Finally, the success and future of Joe & Chow's will boil down to one thing—**leadership**. Leadership is what will make all the other steps happen. Leadership, in many ways, is about making decisions. You must ground your decisions in data, respect, compassion, and humility, but by all means, you must lead if Joe & Chow's is to be successful.

Once I finished, I sat there staring at the pieces of paper, still trying to figure it all out. Had I found George's notes just before falling asleep?

I looked out the window to see the sun peeking over the horizon. My mind was flooded with ideas, but I wasn't sure where to begin. Somehow, I had to formulate my thoughts into a plan by Wednesday. I looked over at the pages of a flip chart I'd been scribbling in, then looked back at George's notes where they lay on my desk. Suddenly, the answer came to me. Why hadn't I seen it before? George had given me the framework I needed to start Joe & Chow's, and the story of the farmer was a reminder! Within the eight sections of George's notes, the words *reason, imagine, clarity, harmony, strategic, operational, implement,* and *leadership* were underlined. Together, they formed the acronym "rich soil"—that's what Jack's story had been about! Somehow, I needed to move Joe

& Chow's into rich organizational soil so it could begin producing again.

I hurriedly called Maddie back.

"I figured it out," I told her excitedly. "I know how to bring Joe & Chow's back. George gave me the answer."

"Uh . . . George?"

"I'll tell you about it later. I'm going to come home and write out the plan for Richard."

For two days, I thought about Jack's story, George's notes, and the current state of Joe & Chow's. I had no doubt that together they held the solution for structuring the future of the company.

As I thought through the story Jack had told, I began to make connections. First, I was the aspiring farmer. I had worked in the corporate world long enough to realize that chasing prestige and money for its own sake wasn't fulfilling. I needed to pursue my passion.

The various types of soil in the story were an organization's operating environment. Just as in farming, the right conditions had to be present within an organization for growth to occur. "Soil" was the culmination of the elements necessary for the greatest possible organizational success—such as a healthy organizational culture, focus, resources, the right structure and personnel, and purpose. Even if all of those existed within an organization, I realized, the danger of deficient "soil" was still there. The presence of soil didn't guarantee growth; it had to be cared for properly.

As I continued to identify each element of the story Jack had told me, I pulled out another flip chart and began to outline my thoughts on its pages.

Path

Imagine a covered wagon on the Oregon Trail. The wagon is loaded down, slow, and difficult to navigate, since the wheels are stuck in the ruts that have developed in the path over time.

PATH:

Marked by <u>Inflexibility</u> — [Policies, Practices, Methods, Procedures, etc.

"THIS IS THE WAY WE HAVE ALWAYS DONE IT."

Culture doesn't allow for innovation.

└─ organization stays in the rut & does things the same way.

‡ BEST PRACTICES!

— Ruts can occur over time or be imported as a philosophy by new leadership.

— There is a comfort level with performance.

— Little organizational dimension.

— <u>Perceived</u> security.

OREGON TRAIL MENTALITY

— Slow moving

— Difficult to navigate around roadblocks

— Consistent & constant traffic over the same area

- Prescribed?
- Rote
- Mature industry

- Comfort
- Ignore competition
- Insular

- ?

A primary characteristic of organizational soil symbolized by the path is inflexibility. Just like ruts, inflexibility is developed by constant traffic over the same area.

When an organization is marked by inflexibility—in policies, practices, or strategies—it becomes challenging to move beyond the ruts to change direction or market position.

Path soil, therefore, is redundant, restrictive, and confined by a narrow structure that limits the organization's ability and desire to improve. It is distinguished by the mantra "This is the way we've always done it." As a result, creativity is restricted, decisions become rote, and the culture doesn't allow for innovation. The implementation of industry best practices doesn't even enter the conversation.

Ruts can occur in an organization over time or be imported by new leadership. Since it is easier for a culture to regress than progress, a path philosophy is likely to change organizational cultures for the worse. Such a philosophy will take a drastic toll not only on the organization's operational effectiveness but also on staff morale.

Another characteristic of organizations functioning within a path landscape is that staff members are so comfortable with the company's current performance that they effectively ignore the competition and even the market. In such organizations, there is a shared belief that the customer base and market position will always be there, and thus there is no need to change. There is great potential for groupthink to develop. Even in the face of a downturn in sales or performance, team members believe things will be "okay" and that any such trend is a blip that will naturally right itself. This leads to a false sense of security.

It is possible that some organizations and leaders might choose to operate within the path because it is comfortable for them. In a mature industry, it is likely that many organizations will function within the path and follow one another so that market position and size don't change often for any of them.

Rocky Soil:

All Talk, No Action   &   **Too Much, Too Often**

- receptive
- desires to do something
- wants to advance
  BUT all talk, no action
- lots of planning but
  lack of buy-in
- plans are not
  operationalized

- always chasing the
  next big strategy!
- constantly changing
- no staying power
- strategies can't sink in
  & take root
- lack of institutional
  or leadership
  commitment

N^{th} Degree— must navigate between Path
& Rocky Soil

- The balance between Never Changing
  & Ever Changing— (N^{th})

Rocky Soil

There are two primary profiles for organizations operating in rocky soil.

All Talk, No Action

This profile represents an organization that is receptive to advancement. Leaders envision a brighter future and facilitate conversation to foster innovations and improvements.

But there is one fatal flaw in this profile: the organization is all talk and no action. The organization engages in many conversations related to progress, but the ideas are never applied. At times, there are even task forces established, but they lack sufficient institutional willpower to carry out the ideas. When ideas or strategies attempt to take root in rocky soil, they die for lack of buy-in; no one truly commits to them because everyone knows the organization lacks the dedication to see them through to completion.

Whatever plans are made, they stay at the planning level and are not operationalized. The plans do not guide decision making as they should, nor do they guide budget allocation. It is impossible to implement a plan without the necessary resources. Ultimately, leadership fails to make the decisions that can move an organization forward.

In this profile, the rocks that litter the organizational landscape and inhibit the organization's effectiveness are created by empty promises, false starts, and unrealized plans. Since ideas never hit the operational level, plans are unable to take root. Strategic planning is meaningless without implementation.

Too Much, Too Often

This profile represents an organization that also wants to do great things and advance the organization. The challenge, however, is that the leadership is always chasing the "next big strategy." Rocky soil develops because of a focus that is constantly shifting to the latest management, marketing, or operating fad.

The rocks that litter this organizational landscape are reminders of the failed attempts at one strategy, idea, or fad after the next. The organization does not allow a given strategy time to take root before it rips up the organizational soil and replants something new.

Furthermore, leaders in this sort of organization can lose focus by attempting to broaden the mission by adding new product lines or services, acquiring additional companies, or constantly turning over new staff members who are recruited for their experience with new strategies or systems.

Overall, this profile describes a company that spreads itself too thin. Since the organization always is resting in shallow soil, the external environment and competitors can be so harsh that a given idea or strategy can easily wither away. There would be a greater opportunity for success if a particular strategy was nurtured by commitment, structure, and resources.

Is it difficult to clear the soil of rocks? Yes. New leadership can establish new ways of operating, but it takes a lot of hard work and will stretch the organizational culture and capacity.

Although rocky soil can definitely restrict the organization from moving forward, organizations should not be totally devoid of rocks. *Some* rocks across the institutional landscape are a good thing; they indicate that the organization is thinking, exploring, and fostering a culture of innovation and industry-shaping ideas. To take full advantage of the various ideas and strategies, though, the organization must move beyond ideas and focus on implementing, sustaining, measuring, and adapting its approach. In all things, a leader must strike a delicate balance between an organization ever changing and never changing.

Weeds

Within the organizational landscape, weeds represent non-mission-related activities, strategies, and operations. They consume resources that deprive more mission-centered efforts of the support they need.

WEEDS:

Weeds represent non-mission-related activities,
    strategies, directions, operations, etc.

LIFE SUCKERS! CONSUME RESOURCES

    - must weed the organization's landscape

✡ Could be planted or could even be external
    regulations and policies

- weeds can develop over time   - "pet" projects?

      Prioritization / making the hard decision

      Weeds prevent success / at least greater
        performance & fulfilling the mission

It is possible for intrusive programs to begin with mission-centered purposes, but over time, as the organization develops, their impact on the organization's mission lessens. Finally, there comes a point at which, if the programs were eliminated, their absence wouldn't affect the fulfillment of the mission. They may be good programs, but if they are not central to the mission, they are distractions.

There is another type of organizational weed that is more invasive than the self-planted variety. These weeds are imposed on the organization as external regulations and policies that consume energy and resources. Designed to protect consumers, the environment, or even to comply with tax and business regulations, such requirements can have a debilitating impact on the organization and its ability to fulfill its mission.

Organizational weeds can develop across the entire organizational landscape or within certain programs or divisions. When the company is distracted by these weeds, it is easier to lose sight of the mission, and the operations become so watered down that success is nearly impossible.

Just as with rocks, an organization can thrive with a few weeds here and there, but it is risky to focus on "pet projects" rather than attend to the more difficult and challenging responsibility of producing results in line with the mission.

Birds

If an organization attempts to function within other types of soil, its efforts (profits, market share, mission fulfillment, etc.) may be exposed to birds, which represent industry competition.

For example, if an organization is just lumbering along in its operations while faster, more responsive competitors are operating in rich soil, there will be little room for the organization to be successful. The potential represented by the seed will remain on the surface of the path so that the competition can snatch it.

BIRDS:

Seeds: activities, actions, efforts designed to foster productivity, profit, fulfill mission

How do seeds relate to external environment?
Seeds must be in Rich Soil!

Other soil types ⌐
will leave seeds exposed.

Birds represent competitors — steal
potential & take advantage
of poor performance

Rich Soil is not a guarantee, though
organization must still be
effective and efficient

However, even if an organization is operating in rich soil, that doesn't guarantee the potential represented by the seeds won't be consumed by the competition. It is possible the organization's operations are so inefficient that once a seed of potential is sown, it isn't worked into the soil and cultivated. In that case, it will remain visible and susceptible to the competition.

Rich Soil

Obviously, rich soil connotes healthy and fertile soil—soil that has the right blend of nutrients to produce exponential returns. There are a number of things that produce rich soil, including missional focus, strategic management, visionary and courageous leadership, attention to the external environment, a culture of trust, teamwork and transparency, being data driven, high expectations, measured results, marketplace distinctives and value, investing in employee professional development, and decentralized decision making.

RICH SOIL:

Healthy, Fertile, Right blend of nutrients & depth ⌐
└── Leads to exponential returns

Organizations are
- mission focused
- strategic
- exhibits visionary leadership
- team approach exists
- there is clarity
- manager—manage
  leader—lead
- working for the good of
  the whole
- data driven
- high level of trust
- encouraged to share ideas
- there is organizational
  distinctiveness
- lives in the sweet spot of the
  N^{th} degree

- Learning
- Culture of
  accountability
- Transparency
- Innovative
- Monitor external
  environment
- No "silos"

3

RETROSPECTIVE

As I look back, each step of my life seemed to build on the next. I attended a private college in southern California and found my rhythm in the middle of my sophomore year when I settled into studying literature and organizational psychology.

Near the end of my sophomore year, a friend introduced me to Maddie. She was a petite, blond, elementary education major from Arkansas with a warm heart and a generous spirit. We hit it off and never looked back. She quickly became my best friend, and we were married the summer after graduation.

After a whirlwind honeymoon in Hawaii, we packed up everything we owned and headed to the East Coast, where I entered a top-tier MBA program. Maddie landed a position teaching third grade. We didn't have much, and I was paying more for my education than she was earning, but we were content with our tiny one-bedroom apartment.

At the end of a long week of classes, I would often go with my classmates to the local diner, where we would laugh about the week's experiences and share each other's pain about difficult classes and professors. Time and again our conversations would turn to our plans for the future. When the conversation turned to me, my dream was always focused: for years I had dreamed of starting a chain of coffeehouses. Ever since coffeehouses and specialty drinks had become part of American culture, I knew there was room for another brand in the marketplace—one that was different from all of the others. I felt I had the vision for that brand. And of course, I believed it was the greatest idea since water was first poured over ground coffee beans.

HIGHS AND LOWS

When I graduated with my MBA, I didn't think it was the right time to pursue my coffeehouse dream. How could I, when Maddie and I were looking for stability? We wanted to start a family, and I needed to pay back my student loans as quickly as possible. I reasoned that I would get a secure start in my career and build a nice nest egg before venturing out to pursue my dream. Starting a business was too much of a risk at that point, I thought. Besides, I had been offered a career opportunity I couldn't refuse.

It was the late '90s, and it was as though our economy's goose had laid a golden egg—the dot-com era. Beyond the Internet start-ups, every company was developing a web strategy. It was a great business model; there was little to no inventory, low capital costs, and minimal overhead. We simply had to generate site traffic to justify advertising. We weren't even expected to turn a profit!

I followed the golden goose and accepted a position as director of marketing for a dot-com that brokered college textbooks between students. I loved my position, and most of my coworkers were like me—twentysomethings who felt on top of the world. By dot-com standards, the company was successful, and three years raced by.

The IPO (initial public offering of stock) was successful, the future looked bright, and I was becoming wealthier (at least on paper) than I could have anticipated.

At that point in my life, I couldn't have planned things better. I had a promising career with good pay, Maddie was teaching third grade, and we had moved out of the apartment and into a beautiful house.

However, I quickly learned that most, if not all, bubbles in life burst. The great dot-com era was over almost as soon as it had begun. For me, the illusion was shattered when Jerry, my supervisor, called me into his office one Friday morning and said, "I'm sorry, Will. We have to let you go. We simply aren't generating enough revenue, and we have to get a handle on expenses this quarter. Security has collected your things and will walk you out to your car."

I was stunned. I stared at him, but before I could say anything, security walked through the door.

I got home before Maddie, and when she asked me why I was home, I said I didn't feel well. I know my layoff had more to do with the current economic climate, but it felt as though I had failed.

What am I going to do now? The thought looped over and over in my mind. I had no income and a mortgage. We wanted to start a family soon, and we were living on an elementary teacher's salary.

I couldn't stop thinking about it all afternoon and through dinner, until I finally dragged myself to bed, hoping that if I fell asleep, I could escape my thoughts for just a few hours.

The months following my termination were tense. I constantly wondered why I was struggling after doing what seemed like all the right things to launch a successful career. The horizon was looming and drawing nearer: our savings were running low, the company's stock was worth pennies on the dollar, and job prospects were almost nonexistent.

5

DIRECTION

On July 4, eight months after I lost my job, the stock market was still in the tank and the economy was sputtering along. We had just found out we were expecting a baby girl, Emma. Although I was ecstatic, the timing wasn't ideal, and Emma's quickly approaching arrival increased the pressure for me to find a job quickly.

That morning, I woke early for a quick shower and some coffee. As I settled down with my steaming cup, I just sat there trying to think of where to get a job. Every company I contacted gave me the same responses: I was over-qualified, under-qualified, or didn't have the right experience.

As I sat there thinking, I took a moment to breathe in the comforting smell of coffee. It was at that moment that the words Maddie had repeated over the last few months hit me: "Why don't you do it, Will? Open Joe & Chow's! If anyone can make it work, you can. I'm behind you 100 percent."

In that moment, I knew she was right. I had been dismissing the idea for one reason: I was scared—scared of failing, of having no idea where to begin, of disappointing her and, now, our daughter. That morning, I began to think differently, not because my fear had disappeared—I still had no idea where to begin—but because I began to have hope that Maddie's confidence in me was not misplaced. The result was that I was excited rather than intimidated by the prospect of taking a leap of faith. I didn't know how it would all end. But there was no way to find out until I began.

Deciding to pursue my dream, it turned out, was the easy part. The hard part was trying to start a business on dreams rather than dollars. Given the state of the economy, the increasing scarcity of venture capital investors, and the tightness of financing, following through on my dream would be a challenge. But challenge or not, I was determined to move forward. ❶

I began by reviewing books about business plans and studying area demographics to determine which part of town would make sense for a first location. I contacted a commercial real estate broker, scheduled an appointment to look at some sites, prepared sketches of my interior design concepts, and brainstormed a potential menu of specialty drink and food products.

The coffeehouse of my dreams was not the typical one that pops up overnight in strip malls. To me, those coffeehouses had no personality. My coffeehouse, I had decided, would be uniquely tailored to and focused on the customer experience.

Although I had always loved a great cup of coffee and believed it should be enjoyed to the fullest, I saw my business as a catalyst for more than coffee; I wanted it to provide a context for meetings with colleagues, chatting with friends, diving into the latest novel, studying for exams, or simply reading the Sunday paper. I believed it should be a place that fostered community. My goal was to make a cup of coffee and a simple meal both the draw and the vehicle for just that.

I continued working on the business plan, searched for a location, and tried to secure a financial partner—without one, I wouldn't be able to move forward. When it became clear that I needed to explore options beyond traditional commercial financing, a friend referred me to a venture capital firm called Pemdale. Soon

I met with one of the firm's partners, Ken. I thought the meeting went well, but I wasn't sure how he felt about my concept.

A week went by, and I didn't hear anything from Ken. It was Friday night, and Maddie had gone to a movie with her friends while I stayed home. I had decided to rest with a cup of coffee and a good book (every so often, I found I needed to force myself to take a break from working on the coffeehouse). I had just sat down to read when I got a call from Ken.

"Hello?" I answered nervously.

"Will, Ken at Pemdale just calling to let you know we're in. We want to partner with you to open your first Joe & Chow's."

"I—you . . ." In my excitement, I had to stop myself before I started babbling. "That's wonderful!" I blurted. "Thank you so much!" As soon I concluded my conversation with Ken, I hit Maddie's number on speed dial, unable to contain my excitement. At least for now, her faith in me was confirmed.

🍃 *Rich Soil Elements:* Imagination, Leadership

Will decided to pursue his dreams. As you reflect on your life's path, here are three questions to contemplate:

1. Are you pursuing your passion?

Sometimes the hardest part of the journey is taking the first step. In life there are dreamers and there are doers. In rare instances, the two are combined. When they're pursued with drive, persistence, and perseverance, dreams are realized and goals are achieved.

If you were to describe your ideal career, what would it be? Are you in it? If not, are you working toward it? If not, why not? Don't sell yourself short, even if it means going back to school, changing industries, or taking a step back in your career to gain the right experience.

There are times when you'll need support from others. For Will, his wife, Maddie, was a great encourager. Do you have people in your life who can affirm and encourage your dreams and goals? They may make all the difference by providing the extra incentive you need to take the first step.

2. Is the role right for you?

Whether you seek a role as a leader, manager, or entrepreneur, you must determine if the role is a fit for you. Do the job requirements align with your skill set, personality, and interests? Job postings are a great way to research the requirements for roles you may someday be interested in.

If, on review, the job in question doesn't seem to be a good fit for you, it will benefit neither you nor the organization for you to accept the role. In fact, doing so may prove detrimental to your career, since you are unlikely to succeed in an unsuitable position. Even as you seek to gain experience for your dream position, you should make sure you are suited for the stepping-stone roles that will get you there. Assessing your aptitude along the journey will help you determine whether to refine your path or choose a different one altogether.

Outside of the job requirements themselves, are there associated concerns? This question may be especially relevant if there is an entrepreneurial element to the role. If this is the case, the job may bring associated financial risks, as well as risks of failure, decreased security, and increased stress.

3. Will you embrace the expectations that come with the role?

Not only must your skills align with the job requirements, but also your expectations for the role must align with others' expectations for you. Once they have secured a position, many people make the mistake of shaping their role around their own interests rather than working in ways that would best serve the organization and its mission.

6

FITS AND STARTS

The next few days were a blur as I began to implement the early stages of my business plan. The deal with Pemdale would fund the construction of the first site, provide access to funds for five additional locations, and ensure operating funds for the first year. There were also provisions that allowed for a buyout after three years.

Everything was falling into place. The next week, I was able to secure the site I wanted for my first location. I selected an architect, and together, we began to conceptualize the space based on the sketches I had developed. I truly believed the design of Joe & Chow's would be key to its success. Moreover, I knew that thoughtful design and a distinct ambience would not only promote the coffeehouse's mission but also establish its identity, give it a character all its own, and establish a "sense of place."

Once the construction plans were approved by the city, I began to move forward with the construction as quickly as I could. Although I didn't have much construction experience, I decided to serve as the general contractor. Every morning I arrived at the site at seven and spent the majority of my day answering questions, providing direction, and keeping the subcontractors on task.

But as the job progressed, it seemed I had trouble with every subcontractor I hired; the workers made mistakes, and the wrong materials were delivered. Because of that, I began falling behind my timeline. Not only that, but I was over budget and drawing funds from Pemdale at a much greater rate than I had anticipated. Maddie was still supportive, but I wondered how much longer she could put up with the uncertainty and risks. I tried to stay positive and conceal my doubts.

Deep down, however, I wondered if I had made a mistake. It wasn't a mistake we couldn't recover from, but given the amount of money I had borrowed, it wouldn't be easy. On top of it all, Maddie was due in three months. With each day I was feeling more and more pressure to finish the renovations, open the coffeehouse, and get some income flowing. The longer the process dragged on, the less I wanted to talk about it. When friends and family asked me how construction was going, I would give a brief response about "making progress" and try to change the subject.

I was one man dealing with the nuts and bolts of building a business from the ground up; I was an entrepreneur. I had always imagined what it would be like once the business was established, but I had never pictured the frustrations, challenges, stress, and pressure of the risks that came with starting a business. Had I known it was going to be as challenging and difficult as it was, I might have continued searching for a corporate job.

Two weeks later I got a call from Ken, who was now my lead contact at Pemdale.

"Hey, Ken, how's it going?" I answered from the jobsite.

"Well, I was just going to ask you the same thing."

"Things are going well," I said, trying to sound confident. "More delays than I would like, but it's coming together. I'm a bit behind schedule, but we should be open by the beginning of the second quarter. You should stop by sometime to see the progress."

"How about nine tomorrow? Will you be there?"

"Sure, I'll be here. They're installing the cabinets tomorrow, so I'll be around most of the day."

"Will," Ken's voice grew serious. "The group is a bit concerned about the project—the overruns, the schedule delays, and, quite frankly, your ability to get the business open and manage it moving forward."

I was silent, momentarily shocked. I had been worried about the delays, too, but I hadn't anticipated the gravity of Ken's words.

"See you tomorrow morning?" Ken asked.

"Uh, sure," I stammered. "See you then."

As soon as I hung up, my mind was flooded with thoughts. Progress? What kind of progress did he expect? I was doing all I could to complete the project on time and on budget. Granted, I was over in both areas, but I was still frustrated by Ken's threats. ❷

The next day, when Ken stopped by the site, he didn't stay long—just long enough to tell me I had two weeks to show real progress and submit a revised timeline for Pemdale's approval.

As soon as I told her about my day, Maddie encouraged me to call George, my mentor. George was retired but had had a successful career as an entrepreneur, real estate developer, and owner of a property management company. George would know what to do. At the very least, he could be a sounding board as I did my best to keep my dream alive. ❸

I called George after dinner, and he suggested we meet for lunch the next day. As soon as I called him, I knew I had done the right thing. Deep down, I knew I was either going to have to swallow my pride or let my frustration with Ken get the best of me. If that happened, Pemdale would assign a managing partner to work with me, making it far more difficult to construct the store the way I envisioned it.

At lunch, George began by talking about his early entrepreneurial years. He told me about his own frustrations—the loneliness, stress, fear of failure, and the financial stress and burden that came with making each project successful. Then he said something that resonated with me: when he was building his business, he focused on the tasks he was most interested in, leaving other, perhaps more critical, areas to suffer. As he talked, I realized I was probably spending a disproportionate amount of time on the design and concept of Joe & Chow's while neglecting the budget and construction oversight.

Next, George began asking me questions about my business plan. Each question he asked seemed to highlight points in which my approach was deficient. However, each question also provided ideas I could incorporate into my plan—ideas that would assure Ken and Pemdale that I knew what I was doing.

The two-hour lunch was over too quickly, but by the end of it, I had an outline for how I needed to move forward. Beyond giving his advice, George graciously offered to oversee construction in the next month, which would allow me time to work on the development and operation of my revised plan.

Exactly one month from the target opening of the first store, we were gaining momentum. I poured myself into the business fifteen hours a day and rode a high of exhilaration as the construction neared completion—and thanks to George, it looked great. I hired staff members, held orientation and training sessions, tested the kitchen equipment, hosted sample lunches with test groups, and put the marketing plan in motion. Everything was a whirlwind, and the loss of my dot-com job was becoming a distant memory.

Finally, Joe & Chow's was coming together.

2 *Rich Soil Element:* Leadership

Will encountered two challenges that are common in any career: first, how do you secure a role when you don't have direct experience? Next, how do you function in a role where you haven't had direct experience?

With the first challenge, identify translatable characteristics and experiences that will demonstrate you have the required skill set and characteristics to succeed in the role. Convey those points in both your cover letter when you are applying and verbally when you are interviewing. Next, communicate to the hiring manager or committee not only how you would fulfill the role's expectations but also that you desire to improve and would welcome accountability to ensure you meet their expectations.

Once the role is secured, the second challenge can be met by developing metrics that will not only measure results but also convey your contributions to the role and the organization. Such metrics should be based on the demands and expectations of the role, as well as any broader organizational measures. But don't stop there—communicate the metrics' existence to your direct supervisor, offer to make the data available when requested, and maintain it in a personal file for support during performance reviews.

❸ *Rich Soil Element:*
Leadership

One of the easiest but often overlooked leadership tactics is identifying a mentor. A mentor has an independent and trusted perspective and is willing to offer insight and advice as well as serve as a sounding board for the professional challenges you face.

A mentor doesn't have to be someone from the same industry as you, but he or she should be someone who has encountered a wide range of leadership and management challenges, including ones you typically encounter. Perhaps he or she has worked in organizations with similar life cycles. Another strategy is to identify someone who serves in the role you aspire to (or a similar role). In this case, such a mentor can be an invaluable guide in achieving your career goals.

If you are fortunate enough to have a mentor in your life, listen to that person! You may not always take his or her advice, but you should always consider it. If you think you don't need advice or insight from others, here's a tip: you don't know everything. Being mentored is not a sign of weakness but of strength. Listen to others, and your leadership and management will become more effective.

Finally, if you have achieved success as a leader or manager, consider becoming a mentor and reaching out to someone who might benefit from your guidance.

DYNAMIC BY DESIGN

As I observed the coffeehouses we would be competing against, I had concluded that most of them built their client base on location and convenience. I wanted Joe & Chow's to be much more than that; I wanted it not only to provide the convenience and quick service that customers expected but also to be a place where they could relax, work, watch a game, or meet friends. That's why Joe & Chow's mission statement was "We exist to create community."

That was why, throughout the design process, I aimed to create connections with people through the design and character of the interior space. ❹

The Joe & Chow's experience began before customers entered the coffeehouse, when they were greeted by double front doors framed by warm walnut wood trim. The front windows allowed soft light to cascade from the front of the coffeehouse, creating a warm, comforting glow from the inside out.

As customers entered and stepped onto the travertine tile, they would find themselves in the living room, where rich leather seating, geometric wool rugs, and wide-planked white oak flooring created a welcoming entry space. Continuing past the living room, customers entered the combination kitchen and dining room. At the center of the coffeehouse was a circular beverage bar. The barista serving at the bar would be able see through the center of the coffeehouse to the front door and to the back through the family room. With off-white cabinets and trim, stainless steel appliances, glass subway tile and accents, and crisp halogen lighting, the kitchen had the feel of a designer, upscale home kitchen rather than that of a restaurant. Islands topped with gray granite provided both a natural space to display products and clean entry points to the registers.

Opposite the kitchen was the dining-room area; its mix of large and small tables made it ideal for working, eating, or chatting with friends and coworkers. If quiet was needed, there was the library just off of the dining room, and to the back of the coffeehouse was the family room, conducive to watching a ballgame or enjoying the children's corner, where the little ones could be entertained.

With each design detail, I hoped to build not just a coffeehouse but a home away from home for every customer who walked through our doors.

4 *Rich Soil Elements:* Reason, Clarity, Harmony, Implementation, Leadership

The physical design of a business is an artifact of its culture—that is, the environment contributes to how people live, work, and interact within a setting.

Think about a physical environment you can control, such as your office. What does it communicate about you to others? Now think about your organization as a whole. What does your organization's physical space communicate? How does the space assist your work? How well does the space accomplish its purpose?

The tools of leadership are multipronged. Some, such as decisions, operating structure, and verbal and written messages, are visible. Others, such as private notes of encouragement to employees, reward structures, and physical space enhancements, are less noticeable but perhaps equally important. One tool that is often overlooked is the use of physical space to encourage features of positive organizational culture, such as teamwork, attention to detail, excellence, innovation, and creativity.

THE GRAND OPENING

When we walked in, Maddie began helping me turn on the lights, music system, and kitchen appliances throughout the store. Finally, I went to the back and grabbed my apron. At 6:00 a.m., it was official—Joe & Chow's was open for business.

I don't think the first day could have gone any better. The team did a great job of customer service, food and beverage preparation, and, most importantly, building community.

The first customer arrived at 6:01 and purchased a cinnamon chip scone and a large house coffee. I was happy to see him settle in the dining room to read the paper; it was exactly what I had hoped would happen. Traffic was sporadic, since more people went through the drive-through than came inside. At 8:00, a group from my old company came to show their support. I was delighted to see them, and a few of them mentioned not only how happy they were for me but also that they envied my courage in following my dream.

There was a natural lull midmorning, but around lunchtime, traffic picked up. Ken and some others from Pemdale came in at about 3:00 p.m. I was happy they arrived when the place was busy. They seemed to be pleased with the design, the variety and quality of drinks and food, and the total of the day's receipts to that point.

Maddie came back to pick me up around 5:30 and stayed with me until 6:30, when I finally left the rest of the shift to Kate, the evening's lead team member. Before I left, I gathered the employees to thank them, then gave each one a small bonus check. It was just a brief word and a small gift, but I wanted them to know how much I appreciated their efforts. They had made our first day a success. ⑤

⑤ *Rich Soil Elements:* Reason, Clarity, Harmony

One low-cost, high-impact strategy for building a healthy organizational climate is to celebrate good things that happen in the life of the organization and its people.

Celebrations foster positive morale and team spirit and are a good way to recognize employees for their accomplishments, both large and small. Taking the time to do so will communicate to employees that you value them and their contribution to the organization.

These times of recognition can be spontaneous, such as when Will gathered the team to celebrate the opening's success. Celebrations and times of recognition can also be tied to the meeting of goals, such as achieving sales numbers for a quarter or acquiring first-time donors. This approach can also serve to drive performance.

These can also be opportunities to strengthen the institution's mission and culture as recognitions are tied to events that directly relate to the fulfillment of the organization's mission. This type of recognition is a great reminder to employees that they are part of something larger than their own particular roles and that their work is making a difference in the organization's ability to achieve its mission.

When recognizing individual employees, it is important to keep in mind that though some people thrive on public recognition, other employees may be more motivated by a monetary bonus, an opportunity to assume more responsibilities, or even by a simple handwritten note. It is important to determine what motivates particular employees in order to build a positive organizational climate.

9

FROM BABY STEPS
TO WALKING

By the end of the first month, we were returning a profit, and by the end of the sixth month, we had doubled the bottom line. I continued to meet with George weekly to gather insights. Ken and his partners at Pemdale were satisfied with our progress, especially since we had a steady stream of business and were increasing sales. Best of all, baby Emma had arrived, and she and Maddie were doing great.

As the months progressed, our regular crowd began to show up at their usual times. They included an aspiring writer who always chose a quiet corner in the living room, a Realtor who met his clients in the dining room to pore over contract details, and a book club that met on Wednesday nights in the dining room.

Many would say that our first six months of business were a success because we achieved a profit beyond our projections. However, I believed that we had succeeded because we had stayed true to our mission—to create community!

Ken, of course, was most pleased with our profits. Soon he called me and suggested it was time to move forward with the expansion. It was earlier than I had anticipated, but he was adamant that we could pull it off. More than that, he insisted that we seize the opportunity to build on the momentum we had gained.

OFF AND RUNNING?

The next Monday, I arrived at the store at about 8:00 a.m. I loved walking into the coffeehouse and chatting with the customers as I served them. An hour later I called Ken and told him that after consulting Maddie and George, I had decided to move forward with the expansion.

When I met with Ken about the expansion, he was more than satisfied with the second-stage business plan and action steps. After a bit of negotiation, we finally settled on a goal of adding eighteen locations over the next three years. Although eighteen stores was an aggressive aim, we both believed that the combination of our concept, design, and product was unique enough to give us the differentiation we needed to make our plan work. 6

My plan passed Ken's test, but George had yet to see it. I called to see if he could meet me at Joe & Chow's. When he arrived, I was working in the dining room.

"Hey, Will. Business seems to be good."

I looked up to see George standing over me, drink and salad in hand. My table was a mess, papers everywhere. I began to scramble and clean an area for him. "Hey, George, have a seat. I hope you told them you were meeting with me so you didn't have to pay for that."

George waved his hand dismissively. "Don't worry about it. How are Maddie and Emma doing?"

"They're doing really well. Emma is getting so big. I don't think you'll recognize her!"

"Wonderful," George said as he sat down. "So, you've been working on a strategy for the expansion?"

As I walked George through each step of my plan, he mostly listened but also asked a few pointed questions that brought out great insights. It took an hour for me to explain my plan, and when I was finished, I felt fairly confident about what I had presented. Since George hadn't grilled me much, I expected confirmation that I was heading in the right direction. But then I saw the look on his face. I knew what that look meant—he had serious issues with my plan. I could feel my spirits sinking and gut churning as I waited for him to speak.

"Will," George began, "in terms of the details—the nuts and bolts of expanding your business operationally, financially, and ex-ternally—your plan is good. I do think there are ways in which your plan could be improved, though. The Pemdale guys are just looking at the bottom line. They want you to show them the money, and you've done that. Tell me, though, how will you preserve the spirit of Joe & Chow's? Will you be able to do that with this plan?" He looked at me pointedly. ❼

"What do you mean?" I asked perplexedly. He had just told me I had a great plan. What did he mean by "the spirit of Joe & Chow's"?

"I mean *this* place," George said as he gestured around him. "What has made this place successful? The location? Low prices? Customer service? What about the mission? Do you really believe that you are *creating community* with this plan? Or are you just selling product, managing operations, and gaining profit? Because frankly, the plan you just showed me was about selling coffee and making a buck."

His words hit me hard. I had completely missed what should have been the core of my plan—Joe & Chow's very essence. I was so focused on saying what Pemdale wanted to hear that I had forgotten that the business had been successful from the start because of its mission to create community. The mission was the very core of the organization; it had been the cornerstone that informed everything else. **8**

Beyond the operational manual with recipes for the latest beverages, George encouraged me to think about the "spirit of place" I had been able to create and consider how I would be able to replicate it. All of my thoughts about the expansion had been externally or operationally focused rather than culturally or mission focused. George was right—if I didn't consider those deeper factors, Joe & Chow's would quickly become just another coffeehouse.

After my meeting with George, I took another week to work on the expansion plan and think through how I would integrate a mission focus with each new site. I conducted interviews with regular customers about what they liked about Joe & Chow's. I assessed our operations to determine if there was anything that was hurting the desired customer experience. Finally, I refocused the hiring processes and edited the employee manual, which I called the *Orange Guide*, to ensure that it imparted a mission focus.

6 *Rich Soil Elements:* Imagination, Strategy, Operation, Implementation, Leadership

It is a simple concept, but if you don't define your future, your future will define you. In both business and life, envisioning a plan is the critical first step to success. Today's world is too unpredictable for you to believe that you can sustain your footing, let alone make progress toward your goals, without staying focused.

Defining your future establishes the objective for your journey. However, once you've defined it, you must actually move forward. As a leader, you are best equipped to act as the organization's impetus for defining the future and moving into it.

⑦ *Rich Soil Elements:* Strategy, Operation, Implementation, Leadership

As a leader develops plans to define the future the organization will move toward, one of the best strategies is for the leader to discuss the plan with people who can be trusted to question, affirm, critique, and offer advice to strengthen it.

Securing a second opinion will not only provide greater confidence in the plan but also has the potential to improve it.

⑧ *Rich Soil Elements:* Reason, Clarity, Harmony, Strategy, Implementation

An activity to determine how informed your operations are by your mission statement is to simply ask your employees, "What is our mission?" A mission statement should be clear and concise so that it can be easily memorized. This does not mean that the organization will lose its way unless the statement is memorized, but a concise, well-crafted mission statement has the potential to shape the organization's daily operations and its future. A mission statement also sets the standard for performance.

There are a few simple strategies for keeping the mission at the core of operations and planning:

- Display the mission. It could appear on posters hung in the building, desk accessories, email signature lines, and certainly on the company's website.
- Help employees understand the mission by integrating it into training sessions. Keeping the mission in front of employees reinforces the purpose of the organization. Once the mission is widely known, it can provide a means of self-regulation for programs or procedures that do not align with the mission.
- In leadership memos, or when speaking to your employees, reference and articulate the mission by sharing stories about how the mission is being fulfilled.

- Keep the mission in mind throughout the budgeting process. Funding is a terrific way to control mission alignment. When budget prioritization decisions come into play between services or programs, ask, "If you didn't do (blank), would the ability to fulfill the mission suffer?" Develop a metric to determine the ROM (return on mission) for any particular program or service.
- Use an outside consultant or trusted advisor to review operations and consider where mission-alignment issues might exist.

11

STAYING TRUE

I was three months into the expansion phase, and although we were getting behind schedule, I still felt we were making good progress.

I arrived at Joe & Chow's at 7:30 a.m., unpacked my laptop, and set up my workstation at a dining-room table. I was immersed in editing the *Orange Guide* when I looked up and was surprised to see Ken walking through the front door. I glanced up at the clock. The time had flown—it was already 10:00.

I stood as Ken walked up to me. "Hi, Ken. What brings you out this way? Would you like something to drink?"

"Sure. Coffee with a touch of cream." Ken said as he sat down.

"You've got it," I said and moved behind the counter.

As I grabbed the cup, my mind raced, searching for a reason why Ken would have come to see me. I was confident that my capital fund withdrawals from Pemdale were in order and that the existing site was still going strong and returning a profit. We were a bit behind schedule with the new locations, but I was confident we could make up the time, and Pemdale had signed off on the sites.

"Here you go," I said as I handed Ken his coffee.

"Thanks, Will. Looks like business is still going well—the place is full," Ken said as he looked around at the bustling surroundings.

I forced a smile. "What brings you out this way?"

Ken took a sip of his coffee and looked at me for a moment before answering. "It's this, Will." He gestured toward the work spread out in front of me.

I was puzzled. "The *Orange Guide*?"

Ken leaned forward. "The other day, when you gave me an update on the expansion, you talked more about developing the human resource training manual than building the new stores." I tried to respond, but he continued, "I didn't hear anything about product development, marketing strategies, or anything else that is ten times more important to the bottom line than the training manual—the *Orange Guide* or whatever you call it."

My heart was racing, but I tried to speak calmly as I looked Ken in the eye. "Ken, I *am* working on everything you just mentioned. But a friend who's helping me with the planning helped me realize that I had forgotten perhaps the most important part of the expansion plan. I guarantee you that the expansion won't be successful if we don't maintain the *essence* of what this place is all about. *That*," I said, gesturing to the pages of the manual scattered over the table, "is what this is all about." I looked down at my papers, trying to regain my composure. 🄎

"Then maybe your friend should provide your funding," Ken said coolly. I kept my head down. Ken took a deep breath and lowered his voice, "Look, Will. I know the concept is important to you. We realize the ideas you're integrating into your plan are part of the brand. But in order for us to meet our return targets, we have to make sure profit is our top priority. I'm not saying you can't do that." Ken indicated my papers. "I'm just saying your focus seems a little unbalanced. My partners wanted me to talk with you and make sure you had your priorities straight. We've invested a lot of capital in this project. We're concerned, that's all."

My jaw tightened, and I had to fight to keep my emotions in check. "Ken, you've got nothing to worry about. I'll nail the dates, and I'm confident that we'll hit the financial targets." 🄎

"I hope you do, Will. There's a lot riding on this deal." With that, Ken took one last sip of his coffee and left as suddenly as he had arrived.

After my meeting with Ken, our relationship grew somewhat strained. Over the following weeks, Ken became increasingly intrusive with questions about the operation and expansion plans. However, I hit every performance benchmark Pemdale placed in front of me, and I did it while sustaining Joe & Chow's distinctive culture.

Finally, we were ready to open our third coffeehouse. There had certainly been struggles along the way at almost every level. Still, though I was the primary general contractor, designer, project manager, and architect, we opened on schedule.

9 *Rich Soil Elements:* Harmony, Implementation, Leadership

When you go public with your plans, there will likely be resistance or pushback, perhaps even from those closest to you. Remain confident in your ideas—if you don't believe in them, neither will others.

You will certainly encounter such resistance in a professional setting, but you may also face it in your personal life. If you have dreams, find people who encourage you to pursue them with solid reason and wisdom.

In a professional setting, resistance may be either direct or passive. Whatever the case, remain resolute in your position while keeping an open mind to constructive criticisms that may show you ways to improve.

In the end, believe, resource, and move forward. There will be risks that come with putting your dreams out there, but there are far greater risks to not voicing them, including unfulfilled dreams, diminished performance, and loss of market share.

Rich Soil Element: **Leadership**

Don't take criticism personally. When you are criticized, take a step back and assess the comments to determine if they contain any valuable perspectives you may have overlooked.

Confident leaders know how to respond well to frustrating situations. You can't be a leader and not have someone raise questions about a plan, strategy, or idea you are seeking to implement. Keep in mind that how you respond to criticism may dictate the ultimate outcome. If you respond negatively, you could impair the relationship so that no matter how good your plan is, key partners or team members may withhold the support you need to accomplish your goals. The ability to maintain an even-keeled demeanor is an essential leadership skill.

12

THE THIRD OPENING

Our third coffeehouse's grand opening came just before Thanksgiving. The store was packed with people as soon as we opened the doors, and we had a steady flow of customers all day. This location was nestled in a shopping complex filled with unique specialty shops anchored by national chains, as well as upper-scale apartment complexes and a corporate business park within a two-mile radius. It was a perfect autumn morning; I couldn't have asked for a better day for a grand opening.

I had been working the center beverage bar for a few hours when I saw Maddie and Emma walk through the door. Maddie was more beautiful than ever as she carried Emma on her hip. As soon as Emma saw me, she broke into a huge smile, clapped her hands together, and squealed. Her reaction was priceless. No matter what happened that day, seeing Emma's smile put everything else in perspective.

I took a break for a quick lunch with Maddie and Emma. I always appreciated the opportunity to sit for a moment and experience the atmosphere that Joe & Chow's was all about. We found a little corner where Maddie and I could catch up with each other a bit. I had been working overtime since we began the expansion, and the opening week of a new coffeehouse always added new demands to my schedule.

As we finished our meal, I glanced at my watch. "Oh, it's 12:40. Ken was supposed to be here at 12:30. I need to go look for him."

I made my way back through the coffeehouse, shaking a few hands and answering customers' questions, and finally found Ken sitting at a corner table in the family room with a coffee in hand, observing the activity around him.

"Hi, Ken. I didn't see you come in. I see you have a drink. Would you like anything to eat?" I asked.

"No, that's okay. I can't stay long. Looks like another great opening, Will. Good job on the promo and making it happen. How did the other two sites do this week?"

Nothing like diving right into business, I thought. "JC1 did well and is running ahead of projections. JC2 is a bit under, but it isn't too far off."

"Is that your goal?" Ken asked coldly. "To not be 'too far' off track? Where are you with the planned openings for next quarter?"

His attitude was getting to me. "No. It's true that JC2 isn't meeting projections, but I believe it will by the end of the quarter. I know what we have to do for the bottom line. We're on schedule for the openings. I've signed lease agreements for six of the eight that we are going to open this next year and have three openings planned for the first quarter."

"Well, I hope you continue to remember the bottom line and focus on it," Ken said. "My partners have been talking, and we believe there are a few changes that could be made that would allow us to have a better shot at meeting the target margins."

"What kinds of changes?" I was getting a bit frustrated with Ken's constant talk of the bottom line. I knew Pemdale was the majority investor, but I was the managing partner, and the business was my concept. The brand had been working. Why would they want to change it?

"There are a few things I think we could do now," Ken said firmly. "First, I'm not sure you need to devote so much attention on the details of the design, layout, and furnishings. Our cost per square foot is quite a bit higher than the national average for this concept. Second, I think it would be beneficial to have more centralized decision making and control as we continue to grow. Third, I think we need to push more product, and at a different price point. I know you want the coffeehouses to focus on 'creating community,' but my partners are more focused on creating profit."

I tried to mask my initial reaction to Ken's comments. Every idea he had mentioned went against the grain of what Joe & Chow's was all about. Deep inside, I believed that the steps he had outlined would kill the soul of the business.

But instead of telling Ken as much, I took a breath and responded calmly. "I'm always open to new thoughts and ideas. Let me think about what you've said, and maybe we could meet about it next week. Does that work for you?"

Ken's expression was unsympathetic. "It does. But, Will, I hope you don't think these are just suggestions. They're a bit more than that. Shoot me an email and we'll try to coordinate a time next week." With that, Ken rose from the table and walked out.

I sat there for a few moments, stunned. My sureness about Pemdale's support for my vision of Joe & Chow's had taken a serious hit.

13

EXPANSION

A year later, near the end of our second year of operation, I was in the final stages of opening our ninth store. As I looked back on the last two years, there was no way I could have imagined all that we would experience. As our footprint had grown, new challenges had arisen.

First, there was the challenge of managing current operations while also moving forward with the expansions. Loosening my grip on overseeing operations was a challenge for me; I loved taking a hands-on approach and being involved in the life of the coffeehouse. However, with George and Maddie's help, I had been able to balance my natural bent toward operations with a focus on my role as CEO and president of the company. I was responsible for hiring the right people, setting clear expectations, holding team members accountable, and building a culture of ownership around our core values.

Fulfilling the mission and maintaining the quality I desired was one of the keys to the *Orange Guide*. A prime focus was decentralizing decisions to the lowest possible point and, in doing so, responding to the customer immediately. Since I could not be at each location all the time, I wanted to develop a culture that let employees know that they were a valued part of the team. As such, at any point, an employee might be called on to make what most would call a "leadership" decision—one that might seem above their pay grade. But the ability to make such decisions was crucial to the goals for every Joe & Chow's team member—to *serve others, make things right, respect everyone, and exceed expectations.*

The second challenge was Ken and Pemdale's increasing focus on the bottom line and constant questioning of my strategies. Although I was meeting all of the performance and return objectives, I knew our differences in operating philosophy could very well lead to the end of our relationship at the conclusion of our contract.

Perhaps the single greatest challenge of the expansion was transitioning Joe & Chow's from a start-up to a complex, multisite organization. A start-up is easy to manage without complex organizational systems, structures, or policies.

But as the organization expanded and became more complex, I continued to lean on George for advice in managing the organization's development.

I knew each level of an organization had its own unique challenges, but I strongly believed that if I maintained the necessary focus on the mission, that focus would allow me to properly frame any changes so that the organization was more likely to remain healthy.

14

IRRECONCILABLE DIFFERENCES?

I got home at 10:30 p.m. from the grand opening of our eighteenth store to find Maddie asleep on the sofa with Emma lying next to her. Maddie was due any day with our second *and* third child—twins, Jake and Josh. Maddie and Emma looked like angels as they slept. I bent over to lift Emma and carry her to bed. As I slipped my hands under her, Maddie stirred and opened her eyes. "How did it go?" she asked quietly.

I lifted Emma to my shoulder. She nestled into my neck and fell back into a deep sleep. "It was great," I whispered. "Lots of traffic and sales. I think we'll be able to stay in business another day." I smiled.

"Was Ken there?"

"I saw him from a distance, but I don't think he was there long. I didn't get a chance to talk with him."

I knew that wasn't the answer Maddie was looking for. She had been hoping things would be different now that we had achieved the goals we had established three years earlier. On the one hand, I could see her point. The fact that we were able to open eighteen stores in a three-year period told me a few things: first, there was a demand for what Joe & Chow's offered in both product and experience. Second, since we had opened so many stores while meeting deadlines and profit targets in an unfavorable economic climate, and in a crowded sector of the marketplace, we had succeeded in capitalizing on the opportunity to meet that demand.

However, at the end of the day, it was a business, and with business partners, there is always the possibility of diverging priorities and philosophies. Joe & Chow's performed well for Pemdale, but we weren't their most productive partner in terms of margin. I sensed they were ready to move beyond Joe & Chow's and refocus their funds on a partner with greater potential for producing the profit they wanted.

I told Maddie, "I have a meeting with Ken on Thursday next week, and I'm sure he'll be ready to discuss their plans for future investment, if any. I wouldn't worry about it. Whatever happens, we've got a growing business and a strong brand identity, and we're turning a profit. We'll be fine." I hoped my words were reassuring to her.

As I carried Emma upstairs and put her in bed, my phone buzzed from an incoming email. I walked out of the room to check the message. It was Ken asking if we could reschedule the Thursday meeting for the following Tuesday. He also requested I bring a summary of Joe & Chow's latest financials, that I re-familiarize myself with our current contract, and that I bring any thoughts about Joe & Chow's next stage of development. Finally, he said he wanted to discuss the role of Pemdale, if any, in the business moving forward. Given his questions, it seemed Pemdale was thinking expansion again.

15

AN UNEXPECTED TURN

I made it to the Joe & Chow's location where I was going to meet Ken. As soon as I walked into the coffeehouse, my nerves immediately calmed and I poured myself into what I loved doing—serving and connecting with customers and teammates. The coffeehouse was either busier than normal or I unconsciously kept myself occupied. Either way, 9:00 a.m. came quickly, and I decided to take an hour to gather my thoughts and prepare for the meeting with Ken. ⑪

I cleaned up and moved to a table in the dining room. Ken arrived shortly before 10:00.

"Good morning, Ken. How about some coffee?" I asked.

"Sure, that would be great," he said. By that time I knew how he drank his coffee, so I went to get him a cup. When I came back, Ken had his notes out in front of him and, as usual, moved right into the conversation. Pure business.

"Thanks, Will," he said as I handed him the coffee. "We both know our relationship is contractually coming to an end. I think we would both agree that although we have benefited from the relationship, it's had its challenges. However, you have built a very solid business, and it has attracted the interest of others."

"To sell?" I asked.

"Yes. Charter/Keel approached us a few weeks ago. They're seeking to expand the breadth of their casual dining offerings and may be interested in acquiring Joe & Chow's. They've made a strong offer I think we should consider." Ken took a sip of his coffee and waited for my response.

I couldn't believe what I was hearing. "This isn't the conversation I was expecting to have," I stammered. I hadn't thought selling was something we would consider so soon. After all, we had only been operating for three years. "Why do you think they're interested?"

"First of all, I'm glad you didn't just dismiss the idea—that's a good sign," Ken laughed. "I think there are several reasons: Joe & Chow's is a great concept, it's performing well financially, it's built a solid market position, and quite frankly, our firm's involvement has lent a great deal of credibility."

I sat quietly, processing everything he had said. Ken seized the moment. "Will, you would be very well compensated. Plus, they'll add a 10 percent premium to your cut if you work with them for a three-month transition, then as a consultant for the remainder of the year. If we close the deal, they want to aggressively expand the concept."

I thought for a moment. "I don't know, Ken. I know the nature of our business relationship will change whether this goes through or not, but I'm also sure you would like to move forward with the deal so you can earn your buck and move on to the next project." I wondered if he would pick up on my hint that their motives and mine were different.

Ken heard my message. "Will." Ken lowered his voice and leaned forward. "I know we haven't always seen eye to eye, but I would strongly encourage you to consider the offer. There's too much money on the table to do otherwise."

Ken and I spent the next three hours talking through the details of the potential deal. I found that I was more interested at the end of our conversation than I had been at the beginning. If we sold, I would be well equipped to provide for my family, especially with the birth of the twins, which had happened just a couple days earlier. In the end, I told Ken I was leaning toward the sale.

Ken left me with a Charter/Keel proposal packet, which contained an analysis of the market, an assessment of future segment potential, a summary of how Charter/Keel viewed Joe & Chow's as a brand, and where the company stood in relation to the market. It also included Charter/Keel's projections for current and future operations, a detailed biography on each member of the proposed management team, and an overview of the offer. I agreed to review the material and meet with Charter/Keel the next Monday.

11 *Rich Soil Elements:* Operation, Clarity, Harmony, Leadership

As a leader, there are times when engaging in the functional operations of the company can renew your perspective and energy. In what part of operations do you have the aptitude to contribute? A sales call? Overseeing the production line? Product design? Market planning? Though you can't consistently engage in daily operations while fully serving in your leadership role, a brief change of pace provides multiple benefits.

First, engaging in such activities fires different parts of the brain, which can spark creativity. Working on projects with direct visible results can also renew your feeling of having "accomplished" something. Your engagement can also demonstrate and remind employees that you know a thing or two about operational matters. What's more, it can enable you to build relationships with employees you may not know very well and help you identify candidates for future organizational leadership.

16

STRIKING A DEAL

Monday morning I arrived at Ken's office to discuss the day's agenda and structure. I grew nervous when Ken told me that the Charter/Keel team was already setting up in the boardroom.

Although we walked into the room with the upper hand, it didn't feel like it. My mind raced back to three years ago, when I had made my own presentation in front of Pemdale's business development and investment committee. Although there had been challenges in my partnership with Pemdale, I wouldn't have been negotiating this much larger deal if they hadn't invested in realizing my dream. For that, I was grateful.

When we entered the room, the Charter/Keel team was lined up to greet us. They all seemed very professional; they left little doubt as to why Charter/Keel was an industry leader with the quality of personnel they were able to attract and retain. Karen, the division president, led the meeting.

After the introductions, we took our seats around the conference table. Karen opened the presentation by describing Charter/Keel, why they were interested in Joe & Chow's, how Joe & Chow's fit in Charter/Keel's plans, and details of the proposed acquisition and timeline.

After the overview, each member of the Charter/Keel team described the responsibilities they would hold during the transition and after it. As I listened, I was especially interested in hearing about Karen's management style. Joe & Chow's was my baby, and I wanted to make sure that her personality would fit with Joe & Chow's organizational culture.

I was also curious about their operational and marketing plans. Because of the struggles I had had with Pemdale—especially the issue of keeping the mission at the forefront of the brand—I wanted to assess Charter/Keel's interest in that area.

The meeting went for two hours, then we took a short break. I hurried out of the room because I knew Maddie was waiting on an update from me. As I walked out, I glanced out of the corner of my eye to see the Charter/Keel team gathering at the front of the room. Throughout their presentation, I had listened to what they were saying but also paid particular attention to their body language and other nonverbal cues to formulate a more complete picture of who they were as a team and as individuals. They all seemed to be genuine, and I sensed a lot of belief in the Joe & Chow's concept. With a few people, though, I had doubts about whether they would fit with the brand's culture. But as George had told me, there might be some things I would need to let go if I wasn't going to work alongside the new team daily. ⑫

I made my way to a quiet corner of the hallway by the windows that overlooked the park and called Maddie.

"Hey, baby. How are you and the kids doing?"

"We're fine. The boys are napping, and Emma is finishing up a snack. What's happening there? Is the meeting over?"

"It is going really well, I think. We're taking a quick break. They just finished running through their presentation."

"Do you like what you're hearing?"

I glanced down the hall before answering. "So far I do. We haven't discussed financials yet, so we'll see. Since Pemdale is so motivated by profit, that alone may end the conversation. I'm also really interested in whether Charter/Keel is the right fit for Joe & Chow's. If they are interested in purchasing us, there may very well be others. So, no decision yet. I'll give you a call when we're finished. Give Emma and the boys a kiss for me."

The afternoon portion of the meeting began with an overview of Charter/Keel's expansion plans for Joe & Chow's. They outlined a plan of opening fifteen coffeehouses in the first three years, then a projected twenty-five per year thereafter. Although it had taken our team three years to open eighteen coffeehouses, Charter/Keel's expertise in restaurant expansion gave me confidence that they had devoted significant thought to the growth targets.

As the team presented chart after chart outlining the potential benefits of Charter/Keel for Joe & Chow's, I became a bit nostalgic. My mind began to drift back to our early days—the struggles we had had opening our first store, then the leap of faith it took to move forward with the expansion. It was amazing to look back and realize that it had all started when I lost my job. Maddie's faith in me had given me the confidence to make it work. ⑬

"Will?" Ken was leaning over to me. As my trip down memory lane was cut short, my mind snapped back to the conference room. Karen was wrapping up her presentation of the proposed expansion plans. She turned to me. "Will, are you ready to move into the financials? Anything else you need to hear?"

"Um, sure, sounds good. No, nothing at the moment," I stammered as I refocused.

Karen moved into the financials and started with Charter/Keel's assessment of Joe & Chow's value. She gave a detailed analysis of our financial statements, emphasizing that while our bottom line was healthy, the business had generated increased value simply from the brand created by the Joe & Chow's experience. That was music to my ears.

Then came the moment Ken had been waiting for—the offer. Since Ken and I had discussed the numbers we wanted to see from them, I knew he had to be pleased. The figure was about 10 percent higher than we had projected. I realized that if the deal went through, I wouldn't have to work another day in my life.

Karen wrapped up her presentation by saying, "We believe we have made a very generous offer for a company that we know has tremendous potential. Are we paying a premium? We think so. Is Joe & Chow's worth it? We know so. With the right resources and leadership, and by following Charter/Keel's strategies, Joe & Chow's will be a national chain with tremendous value for the owners and, most importantly, for the patrons who want Joe & Chow's to be an integral and lasting part of their community."

Her concluding comment gave me great confidence that Charter/Keel was the right company to take over Joe & Chow's. They understood the mission, and I knew they would protect it.

"There's no doubt you've done your due diligence and put forth a very attractive offer," Ken said. "We'll respond by your deadline."

As we prepared to leave, everyone was all smiles as we shook hands. Ken and I set a time to meet the next day and fully review the proposal.

As I walked out to the car, I called Maddie.

"What's the news?" she asked.

"Get the kids ready to go to dinner. Tonight, we celebrate!"

Rich Soil Elements: Harmony, Leadership

Leadership is both an art and a science. Part of the art of leadership is utilizing your EQ—emotional quotient. EQ contributes to the ability to know and understand people and their personalities. This includes understanding peoples' emotions and motives, understanding how best to lead and manage individuals, and understanding how to fit individuals together to form a team.

When building or developing a team, it is important to assess each person's fit with both the role and the rest of the team. During the hiring process, it is important to consider whether a given role is more dependent on the person (the employee's personality and characteristics) or the position (the employee's applicable experience with the role's requirements).

⑬ *Rich Soil Elements:* Clarity, Harmony, Leadership

It is good to remember, both personally and as an organization. Remembering can help you remain connected to your core values, provide encouragement as you recall overcoming past challenges, and offer insights into issues you have previously encountered. It can also provide context for new employees and connect them with the larger organizational story—this, in turn, fosters their sense of belonging. Finally, at an organizational level, remembering honors those who have gone before you. This also reinforces a sense of history and purpose to those currently working to fulfill the organization's mission.

IN THE DRIVER'S SEAT

The next day, Ken and I met at our usual table at Joe & Chow's at 9:00 a.m. Never one for small talk, Ken walked up and dove right in.

"I think it is a phenomenal first offer. Although there is significant value on the front end, I think we should seek some level of continued ownership. I know they haven't structured deals like that in the past, but maybe they'll listen if we can identify some areas where you might remain involved. Plus, our position has strengthened significantly since yesterday afternoon."

"Good morning, Ken," I smiled. Though we had had our differences in the past, I really did enjoy Ken's company and counted him as a friend. "What do you mean our position has strengthened?"

"I received a call from Richard Barrington last night. He's interested."

I didn't know what to say—I couldn't believe it. Richard Barrington was one of the country's most successful restaurateurs. He had founded the nation's fifth-largest fast-food franchise and was able to develop industry leaders in most every restaurant category. Everything he did was a success.

"What do you think about Barrington's interest?" I finally asked Ken. "Is he serious? I liked what I heard, and Maddie was encouraged by the prospects with Charter/Keel. But Richard Barrington is a fascinating prospect."

"He is very interested. He mentioned he is ready to pursue a coffeehouse concept and that Joe & Chow's would fit well within his family of companies. He also likes where we are with our life cycle."

"I don't know." I mulled it over for a moment. "Do you think we should entertain a full proposal or use it as leverage with Charter/Keel?" I was impressed that Barrington would be interested in my company, but I wasn't confident he wouldn't also try to tweak its mission and develop Joe & Chow's into a very different concept altogether.

"Barrington sent us this. He doesn't negotiate and considers it his final offer," Ken said as he handed me a small stack of papers.

I looked over the offer. It was financially better than Charter/Keel's, but under his terms, I would be immediately transitioned out, and I didn't believe that was best for the brand. As enticing as it seemed to sign the offer sheet and fax it to Barrington, something in my gut told me we shouldn't accept his offer.

I put the offer sheet down. "Did you have any follow-up conversations with Charter/Keel?"

"Only a brief phone conversation with Karen. She wanted feedback about whether their thoughts aligned with your idea of JC's mission. I know maintaining the organization's culture is important to you. That's why I think we need to counter for you to remain involved."

"Thanks, Ken," I said. "I know we haven't always seen eye to eye about that, but I do think it's the mission-driven operations that have led to our success. That's one thing that makes me nervous about Barrington's offer—I would be out. Before we sell, I want to sit down with Charter/Keel and have a conversation about this, just to confirm. I've seen too many other companies that, after they're acquired, do everything except what made them successful in the first place—maintain the spirit of the brand."

"I think they would welcome the opportunity to talk. I know they're very interested, especially since word about Barrington has gone around. What do you think about his offer?"

"Obviously, it's a wonderful offer. However, beyond the bottom line, I'm looking for someone who can move Joe & Chow's into the future by honoring and reflecting its past."

"Of course you are," Ken replied with a wry smile.

I laughed. "Well, let me have a meeting with Karen and Charter/Keel to discuss their intentions for the brand before we decide. Deal?"

"Sounds good. I'll call Karen as soon as I leave, and I'll let her know you can meet her tomorrow. I'll also let Barrington know that his offer is under consideration."

Rich Soil Elements: **Reason, Imagination**

Being mission-focused is good, but being mission-constrained is not. Be careful not to let your perspective of the mission cloud your judgment when there are business opportunities before you. Loyalty is a wonderful trait—unless it is practiced blindly. When it's not balanced by sound judgment, loyalty becomes intertwined with emotion, which hinders your ability to be objective. Each option should be explored realistically and assessed on the facts alone.

CONFIRMATION

Just before 9:00 a.m., I walked into Charter/Keel's office and was greeted by a receptionist who told me that Karen would be right with me.

Just moments after I had picked up a magazine, Karen walked out. "Good morning, Will. So good to see you."

"Hi, Karen. Good to see you as well. Thank you so much for your time."

"Come on back to the office. Would you like anything to drink?"

"I could always use a good cup of coffee," I smiled.

"Well, we don't have any Joe & Chow's to serve yet," she said with a wink.

As we made our way into her office, I said, "Karen, I really do appreciate the opportunity for a follow-up conversation."

"Not at all. I'm very interested in this opportunity and want to do anything I can to help finalize the deal."

Her assistant brought in my coffee. I took a sip and gathered my thoughts for a moment before saying, "Karen, I really only have one question. Is Charter/Keel serious about maintaining the mission of Joe & Chow's as it exists?"

"Without a doubt," she said unhesitatingly. "That's the thing that drew me to request consideration for this assignment. I believe in Joe & Chow's mission and its potential for increased success, and Charter/Keel's upper management has expressed commitment to it."

I felt a wave of relief sweep over me.

"Will," Karen continued, "I know there are others who are interested in Joe & Chow's. We're prepared to increase our offer by 5 percent."

When we had begun the conversation just moments before, I hadn't expected to get to this point so quickly. "I think we're very close," I managed to say. "Could I step into the conference room and call Ken?"

"Of course."

I left her office and stepped across the hall. Ken and I briefly discussed the deal, Barrington's interest, and possible strategies but quickly reached a decision.

I walked back to Karen's office and poked my head in. "Karen?"

She got up from her desk. "Come on in."

As she moved toward me, I reached out and shook her hand. "We have a deal," I said with a grin.

She broke into a delighted smile. "That's great, Will! I'll call Tom and our senior vice president to let them know."

19

THE LIFE OF RILEY

From the moment of the sale, my life changed. As we began working toward transitioning the ownership of Joe & Chow's to Charter/Keel, I experienced a full range of emotions: excitement, pride, a sense of accomplishment, shock that the deal had provided me with enough money to retire immediately, anxiety about how I would keep myself occupied, and a bit of sadness as I tried to imagine my life without Joe & Chow's.

Once the deal was completed, I thought it would be good to take a break before I began working as a consultant for Charter/Keel. So Maddie, the kids, and I left for a well-deserved three-week family vacation. It was one of the first times in four years that I had been able to take a mental vacation as well as a physical one. The vacation didn't make up for the time I had lost with my family during the establishment and operation of Joe and Chow's, but it certainly helped! ⑮

When I returned from the time away, I scheduled a meeting with Karen to discuss the nature of our yearlong consulting relationship. I was looking forward to the assignment, since I knew I could help them understand the cultural nuances that had led to Joe & Chow's success.

Rich Soil Elements: Harmony, Leadership

Time away from life's daily pressures is important for renewing your energy and maintaining mental and physical balance. Breaks from the workplace also provide you with the space to reinforce or rediscover your priorities.

There are many ways to integrate weekly or monthly breaks that afford many of the same benefits of an extended break. One idea is to join a club, group, or team that has a consistent schedule and will count on your attendance.

Be sure to take the vacation days that are available to you, and if you are the boss, do not begrudge employees who take advantage of their vacation days. If you are concerned about a boss who may not appreciate your desire to reenergize, make sure he or she understands where you are on current projects and your plan before and after your vacation to ensure all expectations and timelines are met.

20

PERSONA NON GRATA

As I entered the lobby for my meeting with Charter/Keel, I could see cubicles stretching from one end of the building to the other. I could also sense a very strong corporate culture, which gave me a flash of apprehension, since Joe & Chow's was anything but corporate. I really hadn't noticed it before. I reasoned that each restaurant line probably had its own culture. It made me feel better to think that, anyway.

I was flipping through trade journals in the lobby when I caught a glimpse of Karen talking with Charter/Keel's CEO, Gary Banz, down the hall. Her body language told me they were having a disagreement.

Their conversation ended abruptly, and Karen began walking down the hall toward me.

"Hi, Will. Good to see you." Karen stood in front of me with her hand outstretched.

"Hi, Karen. Thanks for making the time to see me." As I shook her hand, she seemed to be on edge. Her conversation with Gary seemed to have frustrated her.

We made our way back to her office. "Have a seat, Will. How was the vacation?" I could tell she was trying hard to keep things positive.

"It was great. I'm just not good at taking downtime. But that's why I wanted to talk with you. I'm ready to support you in the consulting role, so I thought I would ask what you had in mind for me."

Karen looked down at her desk. "Actually, Will, I just met with Gary. He suggested that we advance your compensation and end the engagement. I'm so sorry. I was looking forward to working with you and gleaning from your historical knowledge of Joe & Chow's." She looked up at me with regret.

I couldn't believe this was happening. I began to run through all the reasons they would cut me out and feared the worst. The option to stay involved with the company was one of the primary reasons I had chosen Charter/Keel over Barrington.

Finally, I stood up. "Well, that's business, huh?" I managed, fighting to keep my emotions in check. "I appreciate you meeting with me. I wish you all the best. Take care of Joe & Chow's for me." ⑯

⑯ *Rich Soil Elements:* Harmony, Leadership

If there is a question to be asked in a business setting, ask it. If you are too afraid of an answer to even ask the question, you have already received your answer—that is, you won't get an answer. Try to determine why you are hesitant about asking; if a request is reasonable, sensible, and defensible, it will likely be received that way by the person you are asking. If you are still unsure, make a chart with two columns and weigh the impact of asking versus not asking.

A good motto is "It never hurts to ask." You may need to ask in the right manner, at the right time, but asking is critical. And if you are going to ask, do it early; if a question is in the back of your mind, ask it. There are times when fear can provide protection, but you may need to move beyond fear once you weigh the asking/not asking impact.

21

NEW CONNECTIONS

After my involvement with Joe & Chow's ended, I wasn't interested in pursuing other business ventures. Instead, I spent most of my time volunteering as the local partner of a national hunger-relief organization called Hope Nation. Most of my involvement entailed serving on the board and supporting the executive staff in strategic planning, securing corporate partnerships, developing new programs, and managing the relationship between the national office and the local agency.

One interesting call I made on behalf of Hope Nation's national office was to Richard Barrington at one of his local restaurants. As I sat in the waiting area, I was reminded again why his restaurants were industry leaders. The décor was modern and appealing, the menu was fresh, and the unmatched level of customer service created an enjoyable dining experience.

"Good afternoon, Mr. Barrington," I heard the hostess say. "Your guest is here."

Richard walked up and shook my hand. "Hi, Will. Great to see you. Are you here to tell me you made a mistake with passing me over for Joe & Chow's?" he winked.

"Unfortunately, no. But I do have a proposal you can't refuse," I said with a smile.

"You have guts, Will," he laughed. "I'll give you that. Let's grab some lunch. I'd like to hear what's on your mind."

We made our way to a nice quiet corner of the restaurant with a beautiful view of the valley to the south. The ambience was classy without being stuffy, and the food was delicious and served promptly. The conversation was enjoyable too. Richard was very engaging, and I felt as though we had known each other forever. 🗐

Near the end of the meal, I broached the reason for our meeting. "Thanks for your time today, Richard. I really appreciate it. I want to talk briefly about an organization where I serve on the board—Hope Nation. Have you heard of it?"

"I have. Food-bank operations?"

"Yes. I'm helping them acquire partners. I wanted to see if you would participate in our "Tipping toward Hope" program, in which customers are offered the opportunity to add one dollar to their bill between Thanksgiving and New Year's. Those funds then support the local food bank."

Without hesitation Richard said, "We can do that. Let's start with one of my concept restaurants before extending it to all of them. I'd like to see how it works first. Beyond that, I'll commit to an additional $25,000 a year. I've known about the organization for a while and believe in the work you're doing. I've just never been asked to participate before."

"Wow, Richard, that's great. I really appreciate it. Just let me know who on your senior leadership team we should work through and we'll get it set up. I really appreciate you making the time to see me today." I began to put my notes back in my portfolio and reached across the table to shake his hand.

"It's great doing business with you, Will. You know, when I was looking at acquiring Joe & Chow's, I believed in your mission and felt with the right system and structure, the business could have a national footprint. Unfortunately, from what I understand, Charter/Keel is losing its way a bit with Joe and Chow's. Have you been following it?"

"Only what I read in the paper. They pushed me out shortly after the acquisition, so I haven't really been involved in the expansion. It does seem like they are going in two different directions, though—aggressive expansion and declining same-store sales."

"That's what I understand. Who knows what could have been had you said yes to my offer?" Richard said jokingly as he rose from the table.

As I walked out, I wasn't quite sure what to make about the last part of our conversation, but it reinforced my nagging suspicion that I had made the wrong decision in selling to Charter/Keel.

 *Rich Soil Element:* Leadership

Relationships and business connections often come back around. Treat them as if they will.

22

A LOSS

I became increasingly involved in Hope Nation and found myself working with the organization almost every day. I became so immersed in the operations that the national office asked me to serve on the national board. I was honored by the request and accepted. It meant a monthly trip to Chicago, but it gave me an even greater role in the organization and allowed me to use some of the leadership skills I had developed at Joe & Chow's.

On the morning of my third national board meeting, I stopped by the vice president for operations' office to discuss a few reports, then made my way to the boardroom for the first session. Just as I had taken my seat and begun talking with some of the other members, I felt my phone buzz. I looked down and saw that Maddie was calling me. The meeting was beginning, so I silenced the call and turned my attention to the meeting. After about thirty seconds I felt a second buzz on my hip. She had left me a message. That was unusual. I stepped into the hall to listen to the voice mail.

"Hey, babe. Call me as soon as you can, okay? I'm at home." Maddie's voice didn't sound as upbeat as usual. My stomach churned as I dialed the house. Something was wrong.

Maddie answered with a heavy voice. "Hey, Will."

"Hi, honey, what's up? Is something wrong?"

"I just got a call from Beth. . . . George had a heart attack." Her voice broke. "He's gone, Will."

23

A BUBBLE BURST

George's funeral was a beautiful service, but it reminded me how much I already missed him. When it was over, I sat in the church for a while, remembering everything that George had done for me as both a business mentor and a friend.

I finally pulled myself up and made my way outside. The sun was bright and the air was crisp as I walked out of the doors of the church. As I slid into the car, I decided it was time to do something I hadn't done in three years—visit a Joe & Chow's.

I pulled out of the parking lot and headed toward the closest Joe & Chow's, at the corner of Hill and Vine. I remembered when this location first opened; it was the jewel of the chain and quickly became the highest-producing location. Although I had read of the recent challenges with Joe & Chow's performance, I had no doubt that this location would still be a top performer.

My confidence was shattered as soon as I approached the store, however. The entry to the Joe & Chow's experience was designed to engage the senses and set the bar for quality, service, and attention to detail. What I found instead was a tired, neglected facade. The windows were dirty and spotted, the welcome mats were covered with leaves and pine needles, and the wood on the door was weathered and worn.

As I made my way inside, the prospects didn't improve. The window blinds were askew, the furniture was out of place, the products were not placed crisply on the shelves, and there were many gaps in the merchandise. Music was playing, but it sounded more fitting for a club than a coffeehouse. I couldn't believe what I was seeing. This wasn't the Joe & Chow's I knew; it was almost unrecognizable to me.

I walked up to the center bar to order a coffee. Although there were only a handful of customers in the coffeehouse, the place seemed overstaffed, and most of the employees appeared to be high school students. It was obvious the company was trying to drive the bottom line rather than ensure that career professionals were on every shift.

No one was staffing the center bar. Out of habit, I looked down at my watch to see how long it would take for someone to greet me and take my order. As I stood there, I was surprised to see the crew just standing at the kitchen counter, enjoying what obviously was an engaging conversation. After a minute, I found myself getting exasperated. I was about to walk out when one of the crew members looked in my direction and, without greeting me, waved me over instead of coming to me.

I walked over and placed my hands on the counter to find my fingers resting on a sticky substance. I pulled my hands away and found that two of the employees had left, leaving one young girl standing who gave me a bored stare and chomped on her gum as if she was trying to wring every last bit of flavor out of it.

I looked at her and waited for the usual, "Welcome to Joe & Chow's. How may I help you?" But given what I had experienced so far, I knew it wouldn't come.

"Hi, there." I finally broke the silence. After glancing at the Now Brewing sign behind the counter, I said, "Let's see—I would like a medium Soto blend."

She turned around, "Oh, yeah . . . we aren't brewing that. We only have the J&C blend brewed."

"Okay, I'll have a medium to go, please." I was feeling more frustrated by the moment and didn't want to stay any longer.

She went to get my coffee as I pulled out a couple of dollars to hand her.

"Thanks," I said.

"Yep," she replied.

Yep? I thought as I turned to leave. I took a sip of my coffee as I walked to my car. Lukewarm. I should have known.

I left discouraged. No wonder the local business journals continued to report that Joe & Chow's had struggled to make a profit in the last six quarters.

24

DÉJÀ VU

Bzzzz. The sound of an incoming text message woke me up. I looked at the clock—4:30 a.m. Who would be texting me this early?

It was Ken. The message read, "Call as soon as you can. I just received an email from Charles. Charter/Keel is looking to move Joe & Chow's."

I stared at the words, trying to make sure I had it straight. Immediately my mind started racing. I had never thought it would happen, but we were just under the three-year window to invoke the reacquisition clause we had incorporated into the agreement when we sold to Charter/Keel. The clause gave me the first right of refusal should Charter/Keel try to spin off the brand. It also contained parameters for the reacquisition costs based on a combination of operating and performance variables.

I sneaked out of the bedroom and gently closed the door so I wouldn't disturb Maddie. I sent a message to Ken as I made my way downstairs: "I'm definitely interested. Call me at seven."

I went into the kitchen, made some coffee, and turned on the news, but it was just background noise. All I could think about was the possibility of reacquiring Joe & Chow's.

When I talked with Ken, I learned that he had made a few calls that morning and found that Charter/Keel wasn't satisfied with the return on their investment; they considered the Joe & Chow's brand to be weaker than they had first believed. Of course, I was sure that if they had stayed focused on the mission, they would have been successful.

I talked with Maddie when she got up, and she encouraged me to reacquire the business. However, she also encouraged me to think about partnering with Richard Barrington rather than Pemdale this time around.

I thought it was a great idea, and that afternoon, I called Richard. We talked about the possibility, and he said he was very interested in the deal—perhaps even more so than before, since the brand now had a larger footprint. Richard pointed out that although the nature of Joe & Chow's would be more corporate now, with hard work and appropriate support, the corporate environment didn't have to be stifling. **(18)**

We ended the conversation with a basic agreement to do the deal together. I would serve as the division's president, since Karen had changed positions within Charter/Keel. We then agreed that I would outline our next steps before our meeting two days later. In the meantime, I would contact Charter/Keel and get the sale process started.

(18) *Rich Soil Elements:* **Harmony, Operation**

If, as your organization moves into new structures, new markets, or different operating systems and processes, you find you don't have the time or resources to develop it on your own, hire, consult, or partner with someone who has expertise to increase your chance for success.

25

BACK IN THE GAME

I went down to the kitchen, brewed some Joe & Chow's house blend, and settled into my office with a steaming cup. It was going to be a long morning.

I went to the closet to pull out my flip charts—I always seemed to work best when I used them to organize my thoughts. Ken and I had agreed to speak on the phone at one that afternoon, and I wanted to be prepared for our conversation. Though I was going to work with Richard from that point on, I was grateful for the partnership I had had with Ken and Pemdale. Telling Ken I was moving on would be difficult.

For the next three hours, I worked on identifying my next steps in communication, negotiation details, transitional issues, and, most importantly, turning the company from its downward trend.

I glanced at the clock to see that I had ten minutes until my phone call with Ken. I grabbed the flip chart with the points I wanted to cover with Ken. I knew this was going to be a difficult call. ⑲

As usual, Ken called a couple minutes early.

"Hi, Ken. How are you doing?" I asked hesitantly.

"I'm good, Will. Are you ready to lead Joe & Chow's again?"

"I am. However,"—I took a deep breath—"I'm going with a different partner this time."

I waited for Ken to go off the handle, but he remained remarkably calm.

"Can you tell me who it is?"

"At this point, I can't," I replied.

"Look, Will, I get it," he said. "Am I disappointed? Yes. Am I surprised? No. I know we've had our differences. I'll just say that Joe & Chow's is a very different organization today than when we sold. I hope you have someone who can give you the guidance you'll need."

There was the Ken I knew—little confidence in my ability to lead a large organization.

"I'll be fine," I responded curtly.

"I hope so, Will. These aren't easy economic times to navigate, and you're taking on quite a big risk. If you ever need anything, don't hesitate to call."

I knew what he was saying—*one mismanaged step and you'll lose your shirt. When that happens, I'll be ready to bail you out. And* I will *bail you out.*

I decided it wasn't worth arguing with him.

"Thanks, Ken, I'll do that." I hoped it was my last business conversation with him. If it was, that would mean that Barrington and I had turned Joe & Chow's around. The seeds of doubt Ken had sown only served as added motivation for me.

⑲ *Rich Soil Elements:* Harmony, Leadership

When you're preparing for a sensitive conversation, it is beneficial to have a plan to help you stay on track. When you need to be sure to convey specific information during a challenging meeting, use a talking-points sheet to ensure that you do so.

Additionally, taking some time beforehand to explore potential objections to your points will help you formulate well-reasoned and thoughtful responses. This will certainly help in a tense or challenging conversation where emotions may be running high.

NEW LEAGUE, NEW TEAM

After we had negotiated and finalized the acquisition, the date was set for the official transition. Richard and I met almost daily to discuss our plan of action. We reviewed our communication strategy, the financials and other operational reports, and the nature of our working relationship. We then tried to determine how to address various structural and operational changes.

Since Charter/Keel had already transferred Karen to lead another project, we inherited the remaining senior leadership team members. Most of them had been part of the team when Charter/Keel had purchased Joe & Chow's. On the one hand, it was helpful that they were knowledgeable about the industry and operations. On the other hand, they were also the ones at least partially responsible for Joe & Chow's lagging performance.

The remaining senior leadership team members included three I had met when Charter/Keel had acquired Joe & Chow's:

- Alex, the CFO. He had worked in public accounting early in his career and on the auditing team that had the Charter/Keel account. After five years on the account, he was hired by Charter/Keel as a senior analyst, and his career progressed through the various areas of the finance division. This was his first time serving as a divisional CFO.

- Matt, the head of operations and the youngest member of the team. I was surprised that Matt was still with the organization. He had always struck me as someone who was looking for the next step in his career, but I immediately liked him. Matt had been a Division I quarterback at a midmajor college and had been successful enough to get an invitation to the NFL combine. Although he wasn't drafted, his drive and leadership had served him well in business.

- Brittany, the head of marketing and brand management. She had attended an Ivy League university for both her undergraduate and graduate degrees. She was creative and had an excellent eye for design, as well as an in-depth understanding of both consumer behavior and statistical methods and research practices. Her unique combination of theoretical and analytical knowledge reinforced her intuitive understanding of marketing and branding.

The two newest members of the team were:

- Susan, the chief people officer, who oversaw human resources and legal matters. She was a new hire and had a unique educational background with an undergraduate degree in psychology, a master's in organizational behavior, and a juris doctor degree. It seemed that she did a fine job and understood the business model and direction. However, she was still figuring out her role as the newest member of the team.

- Jim, the chief strategist. Jim was a bit of a mystery to me; I wasn't quite sure that he was suited to his role. He had a background in the industry but had never risen to the level of senior leadership until this assignment. Karen had hired him eighteen months into Charter/Keel's ownership of Joe & Chow's, and I heard that he had been hired to kick-start some new strategies. Although the brand's performance was still solid at the time of Jim's hire, it was possible that Karen had seen a performance trend she was trying to correct. Jim didn't have any direct reports, so he served in a strictly advisory role for the president and senior leadership. However, I had heard enough to know that those in authority didn't always welcome his thoughts and perspectives about issues within their departments. **20**

Rich Soil Elements: Harmony, Leadership

One of the most challenging tasks for a new leader is assessing personnel who remain with the organization to determine if there are any changes or adjustments that need to be made.

It is possible that you have been brought in as the new leader as a consequence of underlying organizational and performance issues. This may dictate changes among your team. You will want to address this issue as quickly as possible. If it becomes clear that changes are necessary, try to determine whether the poor performance is due to a misalignment between the individual's abilities and the requirements of the role. If this is the case, you should then assess whether the individual could be successful in another role. However, there are times when there isn't a new role in which a person can be successful or when there are other performance issues that will necessitate letting someone go.

Throughout this process, remember that the rest of the organization is watching you. First, they are observing what you do, and second, they are watching how you treat people as you make changes. If someone is released, other employees may agree with your decision, but they will also want to know that their colleagues were treated with dignity and respect.

27

CURVEBALL

At last the day arrived for the transfer of ownership. Although I was excited about leading Joe & Chow's again, I was more nervous about the transfer than I had been when we had opened the first store. Perhaps it was because there was more risk now than then. Or maybe it was because I was inheriting a team and organizational structure that were corporate rather than entrepreneurial. I also felt a bit of self-doubt. Could I really turn Joe & Chow's around?

When I stepped into the lobby of the team's office, I didn't find anyone at the reception desk. I found it strange that no one was there to greet me when they knew Richard and I were meeting with the senior leadership team for the first time.

The reception area looked as unkempt as the landscaping out front, and the waiting area was dimly lit. The magazines on the coffee table were dog-eared and worn. The reception desk was covered with stacks of paper, and whoever had been working there had left all of the computer programs open and accessible. There were sticky notes posted randomly throughout the workspace, and a pop culture magazine was open on the desk.

If what I had seen in the first five minutes of my visit to headquarters was indicative of how Joe & Chow's had been managed, turning the company around was going to be quite a feat. As I continued waiting on someone to greet me, I walked to the front window to watch for Richard.

"Good morning," I heard a voice behind me say.

I turned to see the receptionist standing behind her desk. "May I help you?"

"Sure. My name is Will and—"

She glanced beyond me, and I turned to see Richard walking up beside me.

"Good morning. Richard Barrington and my partner, Will," he said smoothly. "I guess you could say we're new here."

Immediately she seemed to recognize Richard's name and perked up. "Good morning and welcome. The senior leadership team is ready for you in the conference room."

She walked us to the conference room, and we went around the table and shook hands with everyone before sitting down. A sense of awkwardness hung heavily in the air.

"Good morning," Richard began. "I am sure this is a conversation you didn't expect to have. This morning, we intend to simply gain an understanding of where the company is and how you have been operating so that we can think about the steps we need to take to restore Joe & Chow's to its industry-leading position in profitability, customer experience, satisfaction, and loyalty."

"And you expect to find all that out today?" Alex shot back sarcastically.

"No. In time, though," Richard replied evenly. "We are merely beginning the conversation."

"And you think 'conversations' will yield the answers you're looking for?" Alex retorted. I couldn't believe he was challenging Richard so aggressively right off the bat.

Richard was about to respond when Brittany spoke.

"I have a question for you," she interjected. "What do you think will result from our conversations? How can you have an end goal when you haven't been involved in the business at all, and Will hasn't been involved in over three years?"

"You're right." I jumped in. "I haven't been involved in the daily operations for three years, but I have frequented the stores, and if what I have experienced is consistent across the chain, we have problems we must address. And I don't think we would be sitting here as the new ownership if there wasn't a downward trend in performance." 🍃

The room became a little quieter after that, and I could see one head nodding—Susan's.

"We aren't saying we know exactly what needs to happen," added Richard. "We just know we wouldn't be here today if nothing needed to change. It's our collective responsibility to identify those changes. It seems to me that we all want the same thing here—a better future for Joe & Chow's."

Richard glanced at me, then continued, "Here is how I would like to move forward from this point: although Joe & Chow's will be within the Barrington brand family, I will be leaving the management and daily operations to Will. I have full confidence in his abilities and know you will enjoy working with him. I'll also say that I wouldn't be here without Will and his intimate knowledge of Joe & Chow's in its best days. Joe & Chow's was his dream and passion, and I believe it still is. Will is president, effective immediately, and he and I have discussed what the next ninety days will look like as we assess both headquarters and site operations. I know Will is taking you to lunch today, but are there any questions before I go?"

Matt spoke up. "I hope that when the company's performance is reviewed, you will differentiate between the overall economic influences and the factors within our control. Ever since we recognized a downward trend in our numbers, we became very aggressive at developing and implementing new strategies to enhance our performance. In my opinion, the external forces are the reason many of the strategies didn't pan out."

"That's true, Matt," Richard said. "The business environment these last few years has been challenging. But there are plenty of restaurants that have weathered the economic downturn with success and are now in a much stronger position—including my own." He looked right at Matt as he spoke.

"Anything else?" Richard looked around at the others. No one replied. "Great. Let me just say that I believe Joe & Chow's best days are ahead of us. Both Will and I are excited to be part of the team." With that, Richard pushed away from the table and left.

As he walked out, I said to the group, "Let's meet in the lobby at 11:30 and head to lunch."

"Where are we going?" Matt asked.

"Joe & Chow's on Fifth," I replied. I could see the group looking around at one other. "What? You don't want to go there?"

"We usually . . . I mean, we haven't . . . ," Brittany stammered.

"We just usually go somewhere closer," Alex interjected, trying to give a plausible explanation.

"That may be part of our problem, then," I said. "Taking the closest solution! Let's go to Fifth. It will be good to get a firsthand look at the operations."

㉑ *Rich Soil Elements:* Harmony, Leadership

As a leader and manager, you will encounter a number of responses from employees. Some will be defensive, while others will be helpful. There are still others that will be too helpful! And some will work against you—to your face and as well as behind your back.

Don't let your emotions dictate your response to such situations. Treating your colleagues with grace and respect will always prove to be the right response.

㉒ *Rich Soil Elements:* Implementation, Leadership

Transitions are difficult for everyone. Your graciousness will go a long way in helping you earn your employees' trust and respect.

28

THE DEEP END

When we arrived at the site, I tried to observe the team without appearing conspicuous. I watched for their reactions to what they encountered in the coffeehouse. I also paid attention to the conversations they had, what they ordered, how well they knew the menu, and even where they chose to sit. Each detail helped me understand the corporate culture as well as the corporate personnel's knowledge of the local sites. 🜲

As soon as we got our food, Matt immediately got back up because his soup was cold and needed to be reheated. Alex opened his sandwich to find mayonnaise inside after he had requested it be left off. Brittany jumped up to switch out the honey-mustard dressing she had received for the Italian dressing she had requested. I was simply taking it all in when Susan met my gaze and said, "You're good—you knew exactly what you were doing bringing us here."

I smiled. "Nah, it's just always been my favorite place to eat."

When we were finished with our meals, I began to talk with the team.

"So," I said, "let me ask a few business-related questions. I'll throw out a softball to begin with. Why did you want to work at Joe & Chow's?"

I had thought it was an easy question—until it was met with silence and averted gazes.

I rephrased the question for them. "Well, for those who were with Charter/Keel when they purchased Joe & Chow's—Alex, Matt, and Brittany. Did you have a choice to join Joe & Chow's, or were you simply assigned to it?"

There was an awkward silence until finally Alex said, "I can't speak for Matt and Brittany, but no, I didn't have a choice."

"I didn't either," Matt said. Brittany nodded in agreement.

"However," Matt continued, "Brittany and I talked about it before you reacquired the company, and we both decided we wanted to stay. We believe the brand has a lot of potential, and we're excited to be able to glean your knowledge as the founder. Also, we know Barrington has been successful at everything he's started."

I tried to process what I had heard. Given Alex's confession that he was still at the company because he didn't have any other options, his attitude was starting to make sense. However, even though Matt and Brittany had been influenced by him, it sounded as though they wanted to be part of the solution.

I turned to Susan and Jim. "You both came to Joe & Chow's without any previous connection to Charter/Keel. Why did you want to join?"

Susan spoke first. "I wanted to join an organization with growth potential, as opposed to the mature organizations where I've spent my career up till now. And I had never been part of a senior leadership team before. The idea that I could influence the future of an organization beyond my role was very appealing."

"Do you feel you've been able to exercise that sort of influence at Joe & Chow's?" I asked.

"Not yet. But in Karen's defense, I think Charter/Keel always made the last call, even when we had all discussed and agreed on a different direction. With them, there was always the possibility our decision would be overturned when Karen submitted the plans to management."

"One thing I can guarantee," I said. "You will have influence and authority. I've never had all the answers, and I don't think that will change anytime soon. To return Joe & Chow's to profitability, we'll have to not only perform well in our own roles but also be active and engaged members of the senior leadership team. Jim, what about you?"

"I guess it was two reasons," Jim said. "The first was the opportunity to work with Karen. The second was the opportunity at a senior leadership level. And I guess another reason was that I think I have a pretty good understanding of the industry and thought I could make a difference in the company."

"Do you think your ideas were the right ones for Joe & Chow's?" I asked.

"I do," he said.

I couldn't have disagreed with him more. Over the past eighteen months, the organizational landscape of Joe & Chow's had become littered with failed strategies and countless starts and stops. But that conversation was for another time.

"Well," I said to everyone, "whatever brought each of us to Joe & Chow's, we are here together now. I appreciate the gifts and abilities each of you brings to the team. As we work together, you will quickly find that with me, what you see is what you get. I have no hidden agendas or ulterior motives. I would rather connect ideas than generate ideas. I'm results oriented. I like to set priorities. I manage to performance. I will always be thinking about our mission and vision. I also intend to trust you, the senior leadership team, to meet and exceed my expectations in the way you manage operations. I am not a micromanager. I believe the team has the best chance of operational success when I remain focused on my role and don't try to do yours too. 24

"Even if you can't do so right now," I continued, "I hope each one of you will be able to make the decision that you want to be a part of the team, that you find our work together to be fulfilling, and that you believe you are making a difference in our world and in the communities where Joe & Chow's are located. I have no doubt that each of you not only can be a key player in turning around Joe & Chow's performance but also can help envision and accomplish a future greater than any one of us would have dreamed possible."

I paused for a moment, then said, "Let me switch gears a bit. Tell me why you believe Joe & Chow's has struggled recently. What is it that has led to our decline in performance?" 🜚

For the next two hours I heard many different answers to my question. The group mentioned everything, including Charter/Keel's restrictive oversight, a lack of organizational commitment to current strategies, being outmaneuvered by the competition, the shifting of the natural flow of customer traffic away from our locations, the economic downturn, ineffective pricing strategies and poor product mix, product costs, lack of a strategic plan, an excessively fast expansion, and trying to be all things to all people.

Finally, when it seemed that the conversation was winding down, I said, "Well, we need to wrap it up for now. I really appreciate the conversation we've had this afternoon. It was important for me to hear your perspective so we can best determine how to move forward. But let me ask you one last question before we go: what is Joe & Chow's mission?"

As before, my question was met with silence and downcast eyes, but I resisted the urge to break the silence. I really wanted to hear their answers. Finally, Matt said, "Joe & Chow's means community."

"Community is part of it, but that isn't quite it. Anyone else?"

Susan said, "Joe & Chow's embraces community."

"We exist *to create* community," I said. Several of them nodded their heads as if to say, "Of course."

I smiled. "Let's go. We can continue this conversation another time."

Given the conversation about the perceived challenges and the team's misunderstanding of our mission, I knew we would need to have many more conversations.

Rich Soil Element: Harmony

Meals in casual settings can be a context for rich conversations—conversations in which you can learn more about someone than you would have in a formal conference room setting. Such interactions can build a foundation for relationships that can withstand professional disagreements when they come along (and they *will* come along).

Rich Soil Element: Leadership

With any team you lead, it is important that you explain to the members your leadership philosophy, how you lead, what you value, and what they can expect from you. Doing so will ease frustrations that may develop if employees are unfamiliar with your particular leadership style. It will also help employees understand your expectations for them.

Rich Soil Elements: Strategy, Operation, Implementation, Leadership

There are times when an underperforming organization or department needs a fresh start. Sometimes the best strategy is to offer a fresh perspective to the existing team, ask the right questions to draw out the organization's story, and encourage all perspectives so that you can understand what led to the poor performance and begin planning the turnaround.

Most importantly, once you have heard the story, reviewed the data, asked the right questions, and developed a plan to move forward, the organization or department must move forward rather than dwell on its past failures.

29

FRIEND OR FOE?

After work, I decided to take the scenic route home so that I could process all I had heard that afternoon. I wasn't quite sure how to make sense of it all. More than that, I was unsure about how to shape the follow-up conversations as I attempted to discern the root of the operational problems. I knew Richard would allow me time and freedom to explore those issues. But I also knew that if we weren't able to turn a profit soon, that time and freedom would eventually become too costly.

On my drive, I didn't arrive at any conclusions except that the senior leadership team wasn't really a team yet. I was still trying to determine whether any of them could make the transition to an organizational culture focused on understanding, embracing, and advancing the mission. My gut told me that not all the team members would be able to make the transition, whether because of lack of aptitude or lack of willingness to participate in the company's new direction.

I pulled into the driveway and checked the messages on my phone.

The first email in my inbox was from Susan. The subject line read "Thoughts and Perspectives." I opened it to review it before heading inside:

"Hi, Will. I hope this finds you well. Thanks again for lunch today. It was great to hear about your passion for Joe & Chow's. I can only imagine how difficult it must be to come into a struggling company that was once so successful under your leadership.

I know it will be challenging, but I believe you will do a great job. Your questions today were insightful, and I know that if you continue working with us, you will be able to get us back on solid footing and lead us into the future you envision.

As I said in our meeting, I think a major factor in our downturn was the restrictive nature of Charter/Keel. It seemed like Karen hit a roadblock with every initiative tried. Upper management was bent on taking the profit we generated for their uses rather than putting it back into the business. But Karen was a company person, and ultimately, she didn't push back.

I know you are still getting to know us, and Jim is still relatively new to us as well. Since I've been here, we have tried six major strategies. As I gather from Jim, those six are just a few among the many they tried before I joined the company. I know Jim is our chief strategist, but wouldn't it be better to focus on one or two solid strategies grounded in data? I have some ideas that could be explored to turn us around. But amid all the activity with the transfer of the business and Jim taking us all over the map, I haven't been able to present my thoughts and ideas. I believe a senior leadership team member should be given due consideration when sound ideas are being presented. If you are open to hearing my ideas, I would be happy to share some notes I've made.

Since I am the chief people officer, I would hope that you find value in my perspective and experience. That's why I feel I must tell you that I see some real challenges on the senior leadership team.

I have already mentioned that Jim has not been able to fulfill his role as chief strategist at the level we need. But besides Jim, if there's one person I believe needs to go, it's Alex. Since I have been here, I have seen the results of some of the decisions he has instituted: he cut back on capital investment so that we have been unable to maintain consistent store design and quality, eliminated the bonus program, shifted funding away from both marketing and product development, and shut down the corporate giving program for local food-bank support. I'm sure there are other changes. Besides that, he has been one of the most challenging people to work with on the senior leadership team. He isn't receptive to new ideas, is often combative and derogatory, makes unilateral decisions outside the scope of his role, and becomes defensive when his decisions are questioned. I could go on, but I'm sure you can see why I'm advocating for change.

Finally, I want to say that I am willing to help you think through managing the senior leadership team members to ensure they align well in their roles. Additionally, I believe I could take some things off your plate so you can focus on more important concerns. I know you have a great passion for the business, but I have seen instances in other companies where such passion becomes a barrier to seeing issues and objectively developing plans to address them.

Again, thanks for lunch today. I think you are off to a great start! I hope you received my note in the spirit in which I sent it. I'm simply trying to advance the company and willing to help wherever you might need me.

Let me know if you would like to get together and discuss anything I've said.

Have a great night.

Best,

Susan

I was a bit taken aback at Susan's email. I wasn't sure what to think. I could see some of the problems she identified, but some of her ideas seemed extreme. I had to read her email once more before going inside. 🍃

🍃 *Rich Soil Elements:* Clarity, Harmony, Implementation, Leadership

As a leader, you will sometimes lean on management intuitions to inform your actions. If there is time prior to making a decision, make every attempt to verify your intuitions. If the data contradicts your intuition, you may still base your decision on it, but you will have gained a greater understanding of the implications.

It is also possible to systematize and encourage input from others. The system could be as simple as a comment box, an electronic submission page, or a representative council that coordinates an employee survey, then reviews and summarizes the results. Whatever the system, there is value in fostering a climate of openness and communication. This also increases the opportunities for increased commitment to the organization and its goals.

30

A PUZZLE

Soon after I received Susan's email, Alex and I had our weekly one-on-one. I was anticipating the meeting for a couple of reasons. First, he had our financials for the last quarter prepared, and although our year-to-year same-store sales were holding their own, I wasn't confident in the numbers after what Susan had told me. Second, I wanted to ask him some questions based on the information I received from Susan—questions about his decisions and his unprofessional interactions with others.

I was working at my desk when Alex knocked on the door.

"Hey, Alex. Come on in." I probably didn't sound like my usual upbeat self. I had told myself to act normal, but the more I thought about what Susan had told me, the more upset I became. Alex couldn't interact with people in a manner that didn't fit with Joe & Chow's values—especially when it came to respecting others and their opinions.

Alex came in looking like his usual disheveled self, a pile of papers beneath his arm, and his glasses a bit cockeyed. He dropped his papers on the desk and collapsed into a chair.

"Thanks, Will. You doing okay?"

I wasn't sure if he sensed something or was just asking to be polite, so I said, "Nothing a great financial report won't cure."

"Yeah," Alex said slowly, "about that. I probably don't have the cure, then."

My stomach turned. Richard was expecting me to forward him a copy of the financials as soon as I received them.

"What are the numbers?" I was almost afraid to hear the answer.

Alex pulled out a packet of spreadsheets and gave me a set. "I created an executive summary for you. You can see that although we held our own in revenue, we were only able to accomplish that with increased marketing and higher sales promotions. The bottom line is that although the full financials show we're breaking even, we lost a significant amount of cash last quarter."

I quietly reviewed the spreadsheet. I tried to formulate a response, but the more I reviewed the numbers, the more my frustration grew. "Before the acquisition I reviewed the current financials. It seemed like we were in better shape than this."

"Well, you have to keep in mind that the weekly financials are purely operational in nature," Alex said quickly. "They wouldn't reflect the adjustments and overhead we charge back at the end of each quarter."

I didn't like Alex's tone. "Then how do we change our reports so that we get a clearer financial picture as we move through the quarter?"

"We shouldn't be managing our strategies by the week."

"I didn't say we should, did I?" I shot back. "I just want to have greater confidence in the numbers I'm reporting to Richard—not just the sales figures—but numbers that give us a broader, contextual understanding. Does that make sense?"

"Sure." Alex nodded as he looked down at his paper.

"I heard you reduced marketing," I said. "Why do you say you increased it?"

"I did," Alex said slowly, "but the reduction was of future expenditures, not the current quarter. That decision wouldn't have impacted this quarter. We already had the contracts in place for the marketing and advertising strategies that had been approved."

"Who decided to reduce future marketing expenditures?" I asked.

"Well, we talked about it in a senior leadership team meeting."

Remembering Susan's words, I asked, "Did the group reach that decision? Or did you present it as a done deal?"

"Look," Alex replied defensively, "we had to get a handle on expenses. We were beginning a new initiative every week, and we couldn't sustain it operationally or financially. So I thought we needed to face some pressure. I thought it would help us focus on what we're doing."

"Was that your call to make?"

Alex was silent for a moment, then said, "I'll look at how I can keep you better informed of current financials."

I decided to dive in. "Alex, I need you to be a team player."

His quickly met my gaze with a look of surprise. "What do you mean?"

I didn't want to refer to the examples that Susan had given me, but I trusted her overall evaluation of Alex's behavior. "Look, Alex. I know that things are different with me coming back in here to lead the company. I care about our operational expectations as well as our mission-focused philosophy. For instance, I believe the store's design—the look, the feel—is critically important to Joe & Chow's success. It creates an experience that the customer can't get anywhere else. The stores look and feel different from the way they did when I was in charge, and I believe there is a direct correlation to the brand's performance. Was there a conscious decision to reduce the expenditure for design on the new stores and renovations on the existing properties?" I could feel myself becoming more accusatory as I spoke. I kept remembering what Susan had told me—that Alex was responsible for the changes.

Alex seemed taken aback. "Uh, just so you know, I have been one of the biggest proponents of store design. I realize how important it is to the company's success. It was Karen and Charter/Keel management that decided to cut back on that. Throughout Charter/Keel's ownership, I couldn't produce enough cash from operations for them. I know they originally acquired Joe & Chow's because they truly believed in the brand. But with the economic downturn, they began to utilize Joe & Chow's as a cash creator to prop up their other dining concepts."

That wasn't the answer I was expecting. At that moment, I wasn't sure who to believe—for the first time, I began to doubt Susan's trustworthiness. I decided to move on until I could figure out who was telling the truth.

"I want to reintroduce two other programs that were eliminated," I said. "The food pantry and the employee bonus programs. Each one speaks to Joe & Chow's underlying values. I'll work with operations to reengage our support of local food pantries. If you could develop a plan to reinstitute the bonus program, I would appreciate it. Let's say a plan in two weeks, with implementation next quarter?"

"Sure, I can do that," Alex said quietly.

"Thanks, Alex." I stood up. Alex gathered his papers and silently left my office. I gazed out the window as my mind raced. Had I been duped by Susan? Why would she discredit Alex, if that, in fact, was what she had done? Was this role too big for me? Richard was expecting results soon. How could I turn the business around when my senior leadership team was so dysfunctional?

The intercom interrupted my thoughts. "Will?" My assistant Laura's voice came through the phone.

"Yes?"

"Can you take a call from Richard?"

I felt dread rising from the pit of my stomach, but I managed to say, "Sure." I heard a beep from the transfer. "Good morning, Richard. How are you?" I did my best to sound cheerful.

"I'm doing well, Will. The real question is, how are you? Or more specifically, how is Joe & Chow's? I saw Susan at one of my restaurants Saturday night, and she expressed some doubt about our ability to get it turned around. Is there anything I need to be concerned about?"

As our conversation continued, I heard Richard's point loud and clear—I needed a plan of action soon. I had no idea what Susan had told him. Why would she be optimistic in her email to me and negative in her conversation with Richard?

31

GRASS ROOTS

Although I usually made my weekly visit to a Joe & Chow's location on Thursdays rather than Tuesdays, I needed to get away from the office and clear my head. I hoped I would stumble on an idea that would help me formulate a plan to turn Joe & Chow's around before my time ran out or we exceeded our funding.

I drove to a Joe & Chow's in Kingsburg, about two hours away. It was the fifteenth location we had built before selling to Charter/Keel. Although JC15 had struggled at first, it was a great location. By the time I sold the company to Charter/Keel, it was one of our highest-performing stores. But now the site's performance was much lower than before, and it was trending even worse. 🦀

As soon as I arrived, I could tell the site was in pretty bad shape—the lawn was neglected and the patio furniture was weathered. I went through the front door and expected to enter the living room, but I discovered it was one of the locations Charter/Keel had renovated to a more open concept with less distinction among the various rooms. With fewer nooks for relaxation and conversation, the new design didn't foster community as I had intended. It represented one of many strategies Charter/Keel had implemented in an attempt to increase sales. I had a feeling that I would see many other examples of failed strategy after failed strategy.

The coffeehouse was very quiet. There was a customer here and there, but there was no house music playing over the system. The employees were gathered behind the kitchen counter; one of them sat on the counter while another stood with her back to the front door. It wasn't the picture of efficiency and focus I would expect to find at a Joe & Chow's. The furniture didn't seem to fit together; it was an eclectic mix of traditional, contemporary, and shabby thrift-store pieces. By themselves, they weren't bad, but without any coherent design, space utilization, or sensitivity to the customer, the haphazard design was a recipe for disaster.

As I walked through the coffeehouse, I noticed more strategies that had been implemented with little success. First, there were several large displays for coffee, coffeemakers, T-shirts, mugs, cookbooks, and syrups spilling into the dining-room space. They had also added a space for selling consignment goods. Consignment was great in theory, since it would connect customers with local artists, authors, and inventors, but in practice, the space looked like a hodgepodge of low-quality products with a flea-market feel. Next to the product space were three computer terminals for customers—more relics of failed ideas.

I walked over and poked my head into the study. The tables were askew, and half the room appeared to be a storage, receiving, and setup area for products and supplies.

As I walked back to the counter, another employee, perhaps the manager, came bustling in. The two employees at the counter snapped alive as she called, "Hey, will you go out and bring in the rest of the boxes? Just put them in the study with the others. The receiving room still isn't cleared out from last season's goods."

That wasn't what I wanted to hear. I wondered how I was going to turn around this level of poor performance. I was sure I could do it at one location. But how representative were these issues across the chain?

As I looked around in an effort to find something encouraging, the employee who had just entered greeted me. "Hi, welcome to Joe & Chow's. May I help you?"

I turned to find her standing at the register. I extended my hand. "Hi, my name is Will. How are you?"

"I'm good." Suddenly, she gave me an inquiring look. "You look familiar to me."

"I'm from headquarters," I smiled.

"You're the new owner, right?"

"The old owner who became the new owner," I said.

"I'm Heather, the manager," she said with more pep in her voice.

"Pleased to meet you."

"What brings you out this way?"

"Oh, I like to visit a coffeehouse or two every week. I hadn't been out to this one, so I thought I would make the drive." I paused for moment. "Do you have a second to talk?"

"Sure. Let me get Avery and Taylor to watch the counter. Sit down and I'll bring a drink for you. What would you like?"

"I'll just have a JC house brew with a touch of cream."

"Coming right up," she said enthusiastically. I liked that. She, at least, had the Joe & Chow's personality.

I watched her talk briefly with Avery and Taylor. She must have told them who I was, because I saw them quickly glance my way then move behind the counter. Heather poured a cup of JC house brew and joined me.

"Here you go," Heather said as she pulled up a chair.

"Ah, thank you. So, Heather, how long have you worked here?"

"I started as a barista at the Hilltop location the quarter before you sold to Charter/Keel," she said. "We were all pretty disappointed when you decided to sell. I went through Charter/Keel's management training program, and they asked me to take over this location."

"Have you seen many changes during that time?"

"Uh, just a few," she said wryly. She paused for a moment. "Actually, some of the changes have been good, but most of them seem to have taken the soul out of the Joe & Chow's I knew when I started. You led with such passion and focus—that is definitely one thing we lost when Charter/Keel bought us. They just didn't seem to care about the mission the way you did."

"That's because it was all I had when I started the business," I joked.

"Well, that may be true, but you shaped the culture so that the employees and even the customers could own the mission," she said.

Her comment struck me and stopped my thoughts dead in their tracks. Suddenly, I realized I had been focusing on the wrong things. I had been trying to address the symptoms rather than the root issues. Had our mission gotten lost in the shuffle?

For the next hour and a half I peppered Heather with question after question about her experiences with Joe & Chow's, pre- and post-Charter/Keel. Then I glanced down at my watch. "Heather, I really appreciate your time, but I need to let you get back to work, and I have a two-hour drive ahead of me. I just have one last question for you: when you come into work, what one question do you ask yourself and your staff as you begin the day?"

She smiled. "I haven't thought about that for a long time. Of course, when you were here before, you spoke about it constantly so I couldn't forget about it. But it wasn't a priority under Charter/Keel, and pretty soon it just slipped my mind."

"And the question is . . ."

"'How will I create community today?' That's what I remember—is that right?" 🌰

"I couldn't have said it better myself," I smiled.

She thought for a moment. "I remember that that question helped the team focus and allowed us to develop some great ideas for the customer's benefit. There was a special identity within each coffeehouse. We were the community hub—a meeting place for groups, a coffee-break sponsor for key corporate clients, and the primary partner for all the chamber of commerce events. We even sponsored a Little League team that won the championship!"

As she spoke, I realized that in my efforts to turn Joe and Chow's around, I had completely missed the point. Because I had talked with the senior leadership team, I knew Charter/Keel hadn't focused on the mission, but it really hadn't registered until then. Refocusing on the mission wasn't the only thing that needed to happen, but I was beginning to see that it was the *first* thing that needed to happen.

"Heather," I said, "thanks for taking the time to talk with me. You've helped me more than you know. But I have to drive back, and you have a coffeehouse to run!"

Grinning, she said, "I guess you're right. But it's okay. I know the boss and I think he would approve of this break."

I laughed. "Thanks again." I shook her hand and walked toward the front door. As I left, I heard her asking the two other employees, "Do you know the mission of Joe & Chow's?" I smiled. It was a start!

My mind was flooded with thoughts. There was so much I needed to do—reshape the coffeehouse operations, increase efficiency, improve service, find the right employees, achieve the right product mix and store design, attend to coffeehouses that needed to be relocated, rebranded, closed, and opened—the list went on and on. Was there even time to focus on the mission?

I walked to my car to drive home. As I drove out of the shopping plaza, I noticed something that may also have been contributing to our site's decreased performance—the Faba Café.

I had followed Faba Café's growth over the last few years as it expanded from a single site to the regional chain it was today. Although it was similar to Joe & Chow's in some regards, "café" was a generous description, since its pastries and basic sandwiches were prepared off-site.

As I drove out of the shopping center, I couldn't help myself—I pulled into a parking spot. When I opened the door, I heard something that had been sorely lacking at Joe & Chow's—music, conversation, and laughter. I stepped inside to find that the environment, energy, and sales clearly outshone that of the store I had just left. Our location had greater visibility and longer standing in the marketplace; it should have blocked a competitor's entry, especially within the same shopping center.

I had seen enough. Not only was our performance dissatisfactory, but we were also being outperformed by a new company that lacked the distinct store design, product, and mission we had.

As soon as I got home, I sent an email to the senior leadership team and shared some of what I discovered by my trip out in the field. I mentioned that what I learned crystallized a few thoughts for me about what we needed to do to turn Joe & Chow's around. To get started on the plan, I called for an extended team meeting next week.

27 *Rich Soil Elements:* Clarity, Harmony, Leadership

The idea of "management by walking around" has been a key leadership strategy for years. Although it is a very simple management technique, it can often be underutilized. One of the best ways to integrate it into your schedule is to reserve time for it as if it were a typical management meeting.

There are many benefits to spending time in the field or around the offices, including the fact that it will help you foster a community, encourage others, and establish relationships. It will also help you, the manager, gain a greater understanding of operations, policies, and constraints.

You might think you don't have time to simply "walk around." Just do it. The results may surprise you.

28 *Rich Soil Elements:* Reason, Clarity, Strategy, Operation, Implementation

One of the most important things a leader can do is keep the mission in front of the organization and consider how it should frame operational and strategic planning.

The mission is the one thing that provides the best means for keeping everyone on the same page. Simply memorizing the statement isn't enough. What matters is how the mission is lived out daily.

There are many strategies for keeping the mission at the organization's core. The mission can be articulated and reinforced through memos, the connection of results to mission fulfillment, and allowing the mission to drive budget planning and allocation.

29 *Rich Soil Elements:* Strategy, Operation, Implementation

It is important to continually assess the external environment to stay abreast of industry changes, competitor strategies, and current economic trends that may impact your operations.

Maintaining a broad perspective will prevent you from growing complacent, and understanding external trends and issues will highlight potential misalignment. It is important to recognize such shifts and determine whether the market still values what the organization provides.

32

"ET TU, BRUTE?"

Several days later, after I had spent the morning creating the agenda for the senior leadership team meeting, I glanced up to see that it was nearly time to meet. I felt myself growing nervous as I headed toward the conference room. Part of it was the pressure I felt to make progress soon. ⊙

As I sat in the conference room gathering my thoughts, I heard Matt and Brittany laughing as they came down the hall.

Matt paused as they came in. "Oh, hey, Will. How are you?" Their laughter quickly faded. Their glances told me I probably didn't want to know what they had been laughing about.

I glanced at the clock. They were barely on time, and it appeared that the others might be late. "I'm good. Did you see any of the others?"

"I know Susan is around, but I haven't seen anyone else," Brittany said.

At that moment Alex walked in, followed closely by Susan. We were just missing Jim. "Well, let's go ahead and get started," I said. "I'm sure Jim will be here shortly, but I want to make the most of our time today, so let's dive in. As I mentioned in my email, I visited our Kingsburg location on Friday. What I saw challenged my thinking about our work, and it reinforced everything I've seen since returning to the company—in the stores as well as headquarters."

At that moment, Jim hurried into the room. I stopped and waited for him to take his seat as he looked at me apologetically.

I continued, "Although I do not expect an overnight turnaround, I think we need to align with a common plan—we're not working out of the same playbook, let alone by the same guiding philosophy. I'm not saying things were perfect when I first led Joe & Chow's, but I think there was one thing we had that we lost along the way. Does anyone have an idea of what it might be?" I asked.

Everyone was silent. I waited a moment before trying another approach. "What is the heart of any organization?"

Susan was quick to answer, "Our employees."

"They are certainly critical," I said, "but I'm thinking of something more foundational."

Susan sarcastically shot back, "They *are* the foundation. Any organization is only as good as its employees."

The room was dead silent. The tension was palpable as I locked eyes with Susan. "I'm not contradicting you, but before you hire your first employee, before you know what type of employees you need or what skill sets they should possess, there is a more fundamental answer." Susan didn't divert her eyes from mine. Her lips pursed, and I felt my heart rate rising.

Jim tried to break the tension. "I think you need to know the overall purpose of the business before you can structure and operate it."

"I'm getting tired of dealing with theories and ideas," Alex said with frustration. "Business is business. You've got to have your operations in shape no matter what your purpose is. If not, you won't be in business long."

"Matt, who do you think is right?" I asked. "Do you agree more with Jim or with Alex?" I was hoping to lead the conversation to a good segue.

"Well, I guess I see the point each person is making," Matt said slowly. Once again, Matt was noncommittal. That lack of commitment, I feared, was what had allowed Jim and Alex to shape operations without much planning or coherence.

"Remember when I asked you what went wrong with Joe & Chow's?" I continued. "Why were we struggling to come up with answers? And why did everyone end up with such different answers? I think that is representative of our primary issue—we're focusing on the symptoms rather than getting at the root cause."

Suddenly, Susan reentered the conversation. "Is that what Richard thinks?"

"We've talked about it," I said.

"But have you talked to him specifically about your ideas?" Susan persisted. "Does he think you have the solutions we should implement moving forward?"

"I've talked with him," I repeated.

"So have I," Susan shot back. "He told me what he thinks our problems are and what we should do. I would listen to him if I were you. All his businesses are successful except this one."

I was growing frustrated. "Do you understand that we're trying to correct the problems that were here before I took over?"

"Then what's the root problem?" she demanded.

"Mission," I said matter-of-factly.

"Mission?" she snorted. "That's the answer?"

"I think it's the foundation of the answer, yes."

"And what do you base that on?"

"Susan, that is the purpose of this meeting," I said deliberately. I turned to the rest of the team. "Let's take a quick break for lunch before we continue."

As we conversed (awkwardly at times) over lunch, it became clear that my exchange with Susan had negated the opportunity to have a productive discussion about mission. When I saw a natural break in the agenda items, I said, "Let's stop there and pick things up at our next meeting. Thanks again for adjusting your schedules for this meeting. Remember to stop by the test kitchen to try the new line of soups. I think you'll like them." As I began to collect my papers, I noticed Susan mutter something under her breath to Brittany. That did it for me.

"Susan, could you please stay for a minute?" I said. I was determined to confront her attitude.

Susan sat back down as the others filed out of the room.

She sat quietly as she looked at me, her face flushed. She seemed to be coiled and ready to strike.

"I've been seeking to understand how decisions have been made, who made them, and whether to shift strategies, and I just want to clarify something," I began. "We talked about design expenditures and how those decisions were made—can you tell me again how those decisions were made?"

Susan looked at me coldly. "Alex wouldn't fund improvements. He reduced the capital and construction budget for all of the new sites we opened."

"I heard the cuts were made by Charter/Keel, not Alex."

"I was Karen's primary confidante, and she would often talk to me about things that were happening. She told me what Alex was doing."

"So Karen was fine with Alex making the call?" I asked.

"I'm not saying that," she said stiffly. "I'm just saying she told me what Alex was doing."

"It strikes me as odd that Karen, the CEO, wouldn't have been able to redirect Alex." My tone sounded more sarcastic than I had intended. I decided not to push it any further and switched approaches. "You suggested today that Richard wouldn't be happy with the direction we're heading. Was that speculation on your part?"

"No. I've talked with him about it."

"I'm not sure it's your place to have those sorts of conversations," I said shortly. "Did you approach him?"

"What? No. I'm not sure what you're trying to do with all these questions. I really don't appreciate feeling like I'm under a microscope."

"And given the fact that you disagreed with almost everything I said today, I'm not sure that we're on the same page. If you act this way in our meetings, I don't know what you're saying to others."

Susan's voice began to rise. "Didn't you say our senior leadership meetings are the place for disagreement?"

I tried to respond calmly. "Yes, they are the place, but the manner in which you approach the conversation makes a difference as well."

"How long are we going to talk about these things, Will? Richard is getting tired of all the time you're taking up with your small-business mind-set. When are we going to do something to turn the business around? As it is, you're speeding up its slow death. I'm not sure you're able to lead Joe & Chow's."

My voice rose. "Is that you or Richard talking?"

"One and the same," she shouted.

Her words seemed to ring in the air as we stared at each other.

Finally, I broke the silence. "I don't think this is working out. I'd like you to clean out your desk. You're fired."

Wordlessly, she pushed away from the table, gathered her things, and marched out.

30 *Rich Soil Elements:* Operation, Implementation

When you're attempting to peel back the layers on operational issues, your primary objective is to determine the root cause of an issue rather than identify the symptoms. One strategy for determining the cause is to write on a whiteboard the issue that you are attempting to resolve. Then proceed to ask *why* until you receive your answer.

Example:

Problem: Giving to the university's annual campaign is down.

Why? Alumni giving is down by 50 percent.

Why? Only 60 percent of the alumni mailing list was sent an appeal letter.

Why? The data populating the mail merge only included alumni since 1970.

Why? The "class year" field of the database was empty for alumni who graduated before 1970.

Why? The last database update unknowingly shifted the data in the "class year" field for those who graduated prior to 1970 into a newly created field titled "class year 2."

Solution: For alumni prior to 1970, repopulate the "class year" field with the "class year 2" data and send the appeal mailer to recapture past donors.

31 *Rich Soil Elements:* Clarity, Harmony, Implementation, Leadership

There is both an art and a science to managing meetings.

Science

Good meetings begin with a well-defined agenda. First, you must decide how the agenda will be established. Will the meeting organizer create it? Will the participants have an opportunity to submit items for the agenda or perhaps place items on it? Everyone will benefit from a clearly defined process.

When there is a decision to be made in a meeting, it is important for the team to know how the decision will be made—whether by consensus, vote, or conversation and subsequent decision by a meeting manager. It is easier to establish ground rules at the outset than try to manage different perspectives and expectations during the meeting.

It is best to identify agenda items that require a decision and then, on reaching a decision, place the initiative into a comprehensive tracking system so that the team member responsible for that action item, as well as the team as a whole, can be held accountable.

The meeting will be much more productive and valuable if the meeting manager can clarify his or her own expectations and describe how the meeting will be managed. Clarity, structure, and discipline establish a foundation for substantive conversations.

The following is a sample list of values and meeting standards for an organization or operating unit:

Team Values

1. Be honest and forthright.
2. Presume best intent.
3. Work to foster trust.
4. Always seek to share timely information with people on the team and across the organization.
5. Give others the freedom to work across positional and unit lines to accomplish their work.
6. Maintain and express a positive perspective about work and fellow team members.
7. Do not make decisions in a vacuum; seek to understand all available data and consult those who will be impacted by the decision.
8. Do not make unilateral decisions, especially when the impact of a decision extends beyond the scope of your role or when a decision impacts other personnel.

Meeting Management

1. "Vegas rule"—what happens here stays here.
2. Phone and email usage is permitted on an emergency basis or during breaks.
3. Maintain open channels of communication.
4. Review operations periodically to assess the achievement of goals and provide staff members with opportunities to present reports. This will supplement your assessment of their work as well as allow you to identify and develop leaders.
5. Provide unstructured time to allow for creative conversations about current and future operations.
6. Encourage healthy and good-natured debate, and fully support the resulting decision.

7. Integrate opportunities for informational and educational presentations by senior leadership team members based on each member's professional experience, expertise, and interests.

Art

Understanding the meeting participants, their personalities, and their state of mind during the meeting will help you decide which agenda items to discuss, how long to spend on them, and when it might be necessary to cut the meeting short and reconvene at a later time. If the timing is wrong, don't force agenda items that require team members to perform at their best.

It is best to address disruptive behavior in the moment. When such conflicts arise, it is important to assess whether they should be addressed during or after the meeting. Don't let disruptive behavior or attitudes fester. Because one person has the ability to derail an otherwise productive meeting, addressing issues as they develop will improve your performance and team dynamics.

TURNING POINT

The rest of the afternoon I met with the members of the senior leadership team to discuss Susan's departure and the impact it would have on our work. I also met with Susan's team and told them that I would be their interim report.

As I was walking back to my office, Richard called. I stepped into my office and closed the door before answering.

"Hi, Richard," I said.

"Hi, Will. What happened with Susan?"

I told him about the day's events and the challenges I had been having with Susan. When I finished, he said, "I'm pretty surprised by what you're telling me. A few months ago Susan and I were talking after a meeting, and she mentioned some of her ideas about the industry. I had to run to another meeting, so I asked her to send me her thoughts in a follow-up email, which she did. She had some good thoughts, and I told her so. We stayed in contact periodically, and she continued to share her ideas, but over time, her thoughts moved from the industry in general to Joe & Chow's in particular. At that point I should have told you—I'm sorry. I've always had an open-door policy, but looking back, I can see how her thoughts were shaping my own perspective not only of Joe & Chow's but also of your work and leadership."

"I appreciate that, Richard," I said. "I didn't mention it earlier, but one thing she said in our senior leadership team meeting was that not only does she question my ability to turn Joe & Chow's around, but you do too."

"That's not true, Will," Richard said. "I believe in you, and I know you're the right person to turn Joe & Chow's around. I've always thought that. That said, we do need to make progress. I have tried to be as gracious as possible with my expectations, but I can't continue to carry Joe & Chow's indefinitely. Haven't you had enough time to assess what needs to happen? We need to start making some moves. Whether the issues are operational, financial, or cultural, we need to see some positive impact on the bottom line."

With as much resolve as I had ever spoken with, I said, "Richard, first of all, thank you for your time tonight. I'm glad that you consider the future of Joe & Chow's important enough to warrant the meeting. Second, I appreciate the time you've allowed me as we've sought to turn operations around. I know there is much potential in the brand, and I believe you're making a good investment. Defining a plan based on the data we've collected was the primary purpose of the senior leadership team meeting today until things went south with Susan. I'll have a plan on your desk by Wednesday. I'll include measurable results one month from today, and we'll be turning a profit three months from now."

"That sounds great, Will."

After we hung up, I called Maddie to let her know that I was going to stay late at the office. That was the night I heard the story that changed my organizational perspective forever.

A TRANSFORMATIONAL PLAN

After hearing Jack's story (see chap. 1), I spent the next three days formulating a plan based on George's framework. Over the course of the previous few months I had collected data about Joe & Chow's operations, and now George's framework helped me make sense of it all.

That Monday morning, I worked feverishly to develop a rough draft of the plan and then called a senior leadership team meeting for the afternoon. The senior leadership team members gave me great feedback and ideas, and for the first time, I felt that they understood our focus, where we were headed, and what it would take to get there. The framework from George's notes helped me organize the plan and break it into manageable steps.

When I finished a draft of the plan on Tuesday evening, I was confident that it would not only get Joe & Chow's back to its successful roots but also reshape the company within a profitable framework.

THREE YEARS LATER

I arrived at the Joe & Chow's on Fifth Street at a quarter to nine, and the place was alive with customers. Especially in the wake of the Charter/Keel period, it was a welcome sight.

I walked up to the barista behind the counter. "Hi, Kent. How's everything been going?"

"Hey, Will. Things are great. And I've been meaning to tell you—we are going to host those monthly city council coffees I was telling you about."

"That's awesome, Kent. Great job."

"Thanks. Can I get you a drink?"

"I'm meeting someone at nine, so I'll just wait until he gets here. Thanks, though."

Just moments after I sat down, a young man walked up to me. "Will?"

"Yes. Are you Michael?"

"Yes—Michael Brower with *The Business Times*." He extended his hand. "Congratulations on being named business of the year. I appreciate your time today."

"No problem at all. I still don't know if we're worthy of the award given who the other nominees were, but we're honored."

Michael smiled. "You know, I remember our coverage when you opened the very first Joe & Chow's. You were on the "Best Of" list for new businesses that year, right?"

"We were. It's hard to even remember those days."

"Which was more challenging for you—the start-up phase or taking over the business from Charter/Keel?" Michael asked as he pulled out his notebook.

"Well, they've been two very different experiences. Our current business model has completely changed from the time we first began. As a CEO, you can't engage at the operational level when you have sixty-eight stores. The number of sites and breadth of focus require a more corporate and centralized model that was very foreign to me. I understood the corporate model in theory, but I didn't have direct experience. My definition of success didn't change, but it took me awhile to figure out how to achieve it when I came back to the company. Richard Barrington was a key figure in helping me understand the corporate culture."

"So how do you define success?" Michael asked.

"For me, success is fulfilling the mission of the organization. The mission has to be the focus as you are pursuing operational excellence. When the mission becomes the organization's driving force, the opportunities for financial success are increased."

"And Joe & Chow's has been successful in that regard."

"Definitely," I said. "We made a number of operational changes that led to our success. We enhanced our customer experience, improved the quality of our food and drinks, introduced new and seasonal products based on customer research, and implemented a renewed emphasis on the design and layout of our coffeehouses. Beyond that, we expanded from forty-seven coffeehouses three years ago to sixty-eight today. Plus, we just secured additional capital that will allow us to continue our growth plan as we move more aggressively into the southern region."

"What do you think the role of leadership is when you are trying to increase a company's performance?"

"The first task of a leader is to determine and define where the organization is in both its development and operations," I responded. "This will dictate what is required of leadership. Not every leadership strategy will work at each stage, and unless you recognize and respect the organization's culture, deficiencies, and strengths, you can actually do more harm than good. At its most basic level, though, a leader must be willing to lead. Leading is not easy; it is demanding and challenging. However, it is also very rewarding."

Michael asked a follow-up, "How did you determine 'where' the organization was in its development and how to take it where you wanted it to be?"

"I began by asking five questions of my colleagues: Who are we? Where are we? Where are we going? How will we get there? and Why is it important that we get there? The questions helped bring everyone together around the mission and provided clarity and understanding about what we were trying to accomplish as a company. After answering the questions, I led a strategic planning process to expand the third question through the fifth question. The result was a five-year plan that had the ownership and buy-in of all of the team—from corporate to each coffeehouse."

"One final question for now—is your success everything you had hoped for?"

I didn't hesitate. "Without a doubt. I'm very pleased with our success, certainly with our operating performance but, more than that, with the fact that we were able to rediscover our purpose—to create community. Everything else has flowed from our mission."

"And how does that affect you personally?" Michael asked.

"I'm having the time of my life. What better way to make a living than by following your passion? A few years ago, Joe & Chow's was just a dream of mine. To walk the journey I have in realizing that dream—I couldn't ask for anything more."

"One last question," Michael said. "What's next for Joe & Chow's?"

"We're going to maintain our focus on our mission and follow the strategies we've outlined," I said. "As a result, I believe our growth will be exponential. To paraphrase a friend of mine, we'll continue to sow our seed, knowing that some will fall on the path, on the rocks, and among the weeds. But ultimately, if we stay true to our purpose, I believe our efforts will fall on rich soil."

APPENDIX

The Eight Elements of Rich Soil
Transforming Organizational Landscapes

The following eight elements (see pp. 10, 16-17) provide a framework for organizations seeking to maximize their performance. As you review each element, think about your own organization and its leadership, then rate on a scale of one to ten how you believe your organization embodies each one. There are questions at the end of each section to assist you in your analysis.

If you discover that your ratings are lower than they should be, you can begin the transformation process by using this framework to determine why the deficiency exists and how to correct it.

1. *Reason:* Ensure your organization understands and embraces the reason it exists—its mission.

An organization's reason for existence is its foundational mission. It is foundational because in order for the organization to be successful, the mission must be understood at every level and inform everything the organization seeks to accomplish.

Without a framing reason for existence, the organization is likely to be tossed about by external forces as well as weakened by competing internal ideas about the organization's mission. When this occurs, the organization not only is unlikely to achieve its strategic goals but also will suffer in its daily operations and create a fragmented culture and focus.

To properly align its daily efforts, the organization must capture the mission in a memorable and succinct statement that is both philosophical and functional in nature; it must be philosophical to ensure the mission is fitting, and functional to ensure the mission can be operationalized.

Think of the organization as a vehicle on a road trip. Identifying, understanding, and embracing the organization's reason for existence provides both the impetus (the *why*) for the trip and the guideposts to ensure continual progress. Internal benchmarks, gauges, and data monitor the organization's effectiveness in mission fulfillment (the *how*).

All planning, of any nature, must begin with and be framed by the organization's mission. It is the mission that gives the organization meaning and purpose.

Reason—Initial Soil Assessment

1. Do you have a clear, compelling, and succinct mission statement that defines why your organization exists?
2. Has the mission shifted over time? If so, why?
3. Do both internal and external audiences understand your mission statement?

4. In reflecting on the types of soil described in the "rich soil" framework (path soil, rocky soil, etc.), can you identify any obstacles that are preventing you from effectively fulfilling your mission?

2. *Imagination:* Imagine a compelling, shared vision of your organization's future.

While a mission statement defines the organization's reason for existence, a vision statement describes where the organization wants to go in the future.

Once the organization understands and embraces its reason for existence, it is imperative to identify where the organization is headed. Vision will lead an organization to reinvent core strategies and explore new ways of doing business, and will ultimately foster vibrancy, growth, and life.

Though every organization must possess a vision for the future, the process of developing the vision is different for each organization. The key, though, is to have a process that fosters imagination among those invested in the company.

An organization's vision should be unique. Granted, there will be other organizations that aim for similar destinations, but organizationally unique characteristics, including culture, history, and life cycle, are bound to drive them down different paths. Vision is both ambitious and achievable. It is positive, hopeful, identifies organizational opportunities, and inspires people to act.

An organization's vision can be both quantitative and qualitative, short term and long term, emotional and rational. A vision is dynamic and must account for the changing internal and external environments.

An overarching vision is qualitative in nature and describes the organization's identity and value. This qualitative vision defines what the organization wants to *be*—what the organization will be recognized or known for.

Strategic vision, then, more practically defines the destination and how the overarching vision will be achieved. A strategic vision will define the steps and actions necessary to achieve the desired future. The quantitative vision should describe what the organization desires to *become, see, possess,* and *have.*

Imagination—Initial Soil Assessment

1. Is there a defined future for your organization? Does the vision challenge the organization to grow?
2. Are employees invested in the plan for the future? Do they understand how their efforts support the plan?
3. How will you know when you have arrived at your desired destination?
4. Does the organization's culture lend itself to the pursuit of a visionary future?

3. *Clarity:* Ensure that the organization has a clear understanding of its mission and vision.

Once you identify the organization's reason for existence and imagine a vision for its future, the reason and vision must not only be acknowledged but also lived out by employees. In this way, the goals come alive in those who work to accomplish them.

It can be tempting for leaders to determine unilaterally the reason and vision for the organization. However, simply giving orders and expecting employees to accept them is not enough. Clarity should become a way of life for the organization and its leadership. Although the leader is ultimately responsible for fostering clarity, a few basic principles will ensure that everyone in the organization works together to understand and live out its goals.

First, clarity begins with a shared vision. Though the organization will gain new employees who haven't participated in the development of the vision, the company's success depends on their understanding and advancement of it. If employees are unclear about the organization's goals, the leader is unlikely to garner the buy-in necessary for achieving them.

The strength of an organization's understanding and commitment to its mission and vision can even serve to attract employees and partners who desire to be members of such a focused, successful, and healthy organization.

A leader must utilize verbal, written, and symbolic communication when providing clarity for the organization. Perhaps the best strategy is to tell the stories that capture the soul of the organization and illustrate how the vision is lived out. Such stories not only help employees identify with the organization but also show them that they are vital parts of a bigger picture. Again, capturing the mission and vision in succinct, memorable statements will aid employees in internalizing and applying them.

Clarity—Initial Soil Assessment

1. Does each level of the organization understand and embrace the mission and vision?
2. Does each of the organization's programs and departments align with the mission and vision? Can employees identify how their roles support and advance the mission and vision?
3. Are you making progress in fulfilling your mission and vision? How do you know?
4. What strategies do you use to ensure that new employees understand the mission and vision?
5. How do you reinforce and articulate the mission and vision? Verbally? In writing? Symbolically?

4. *Harmony:* When carefully arranged and skillfully directed, the right players will perform harmoniously.

By now, your organization should have defined its mission and vision and the strategies for ensuring that both are clearly understood. It is at this point you must ask a difficult question: are the right team members arranged in such a way that they will be able to achieve the organization's goals?

Intuitively, we understand that organizations are difficult to change—especially when it comes to changing them in ways that position them for greater success and continued development. In order to fulfill the mission and advance the vision, a leader must not only provide clarity but also lead in a way that allows teams to move forward with the same purpose. Organizational progress is made possible only through organizational harmony.

For example, think of an organization as an orchestra. In order to produce beautiful music, each member of the orchestra must both perform well within his or her individual roles and collaborate with the other members of the orchestra.

In an orchestra, there are different players who play different instruments. Some members assume leading roles, while others fill supporting roles by providing a rhythm or the right sound at the right moment.

There are also section leaders who help maintain each member's connection to the rest of his or her section as well as the orchestra as a whole. They communicate the conductor's intent to the section and ensure that the conductor has a clear understanding of the section's performance and collaboration.

In building the various elements of an orchestra, it is possible that some members just won't fit. Some members may need to be moved within their section. Perhaps, for example, they cannot play the lead part but can play the second or third part quite successfully. Perhaps others must move from one instrument to another that better fits their range and capabilities. At worst, some players may want to be a one-person band. When this happens, harmony is even harder to achieve and such players may need to be released.

Even if a player is in the right role, his or her performance within that role may still be an issue. The conductor must carefully match each musician's passion, skill, and dedication to the goals of the orchestra as a whole. If the conductor discovers that a player has no rhythm, is tone deaf, or is unable to appreciate the music he or she is attempting to play, the player must be removed from the orchestra altogether.

Overall, the process of creating harmony through combining many players and many varied instruments playing different parts clearly illustrates that within an organization there can be *difference without dissonance*. However, if dissonance is discovered, it must be addressed. Neglecting to do so jeopardizes the organization's mission and vision.

For any band or orchestra, at whatever level, there is always one common thread—the score, or sheet music, that provides the notes to perform. The leader must be attuned to the role and output of all sections, listening, assessing, and ensuring they remain on the same page.

In a similar vein, organizations should have a combination of "scores"—a set of plans that enables each department to understand where the organization is going and know how it fits into that plan.

Harmony—Initial Soil Assessment

1. As a leader, are you willing to live with a bit of dissonance in the process of fostering harmony? Achieving organizational harmony is a long, complicated process.

2. Do your employees embrace teamwork, or are they competitive and adversarial?

3. Are there measurable performance standards in place to help you determine how well individual personnel members fit within the organization?

4. Do the various departments and units of the organization understand their roles in fulfilling the mission and achieving the vision?

5. Can you identify anyone within the organization who is assigned to the wrong instrument or playing out of tune? If so, harmony will be impossible until the dissonance is addressed.

5. *Strategy:* An organization's hope for the future is built on its strategy for getting there.

Once the mission is defined, the vision is identified, and both seem to be understood and embraced by employees, an inevitable question arises: how do you bring all those elements together to advance the organization?

You need a framework to realize your vision. It is at this point that you must formulate what are commonly called strategic goals.

Strategic goals are directional in nature. They serve as the bridge from the philosophical vision to the more practical aspects of operational planning. They are long-term plans (five to ten years) that identify a desired result. Strategic goals, when realized, fulfill the mission and accomplish the vision.

Calling a goal "strategic" implies that you established it only after assessing the external environment, identifying the organization's position relative to its competitors, and recognizing its strengths and weaknesses. With all these factors in mind, strategic goals are designed to move the organization in a preferred direction.

You can only develop strategic goals after you identify your organization's soil type. Once you have done so, your plan can address specific deficiencies and establish a strategy for moving the organization into rich soil.

Your goals must complement the organization's mission and vision by recognizing its past, assessing its current environment, and positioning it to move confidently into the future defined by its vision. Goals framed in this manner will position the organization to respond to the opportunities, threats, and external trends it will encounter in the future.

Thus strategic planning yields strategic goals that serve to increase performance and effectiveness, counter adverse environmental factors, combat organizational complacency, and position the organization for success.

Strategy—Initial Soil Assessment

1. Do you have an ongoing strategic planning process? Does your plan recognize your organization's soil type?
2. Does your planning process result in specific action steps?
3. Is your strategic plan fully aligned with your mission and vision?
4. Does your plan account for the competitive landscape, consumer trends, and environmental factors?

6. *Operation:* Strategy is brought to life by operation.

While strategic goals provide direction, operational objectives are intended to start the organization moving in the chosen direction. In the symphony metaphor, operational objectives define which instruments are to perform and what notes are to be played at specific times to produce music. Each note, measure, and movement is a critical component of the whole composition.

Strategic goals are comprehensive in scope and impact, but they are operationalized through various organizational departments and functions. It is critical to keep the mission, vision, and values of the organization at the forefront during planning processes. This focus will ensure that various levels of planning remain aligned with the organizational goals.

Defining and refining operational objectives is not always as exhilarating as envisioning the future, but without such objectives, the vision cannot be realized. Operational objectives translate strategy to action. They are the steps that will propel the organization toward the rich soil it seeks.

Because of the long range of strategic goals, accomplishing them in a single step is often unrealistic. Organizations are difficult to change, but breaking strategic goals into actionable steps with prescribed progress checkpoints and assessment metrics makes the seemingly impossible possible.

There are two aims of operational objectives. The first is ensuring that the objectives are aligned with the identified strategic goals. Essentially, this aspect focuses on the organization's effectiveness—the practical, daily accomplishment of its mission and vision.

Operational objectives serve as the impetus for either reclaiming organizational soil by removing rocks and weeds or moving the organization to new soil altogether. Of course, the movement to new soil requires transforming the deeper layers of the organization's culture, including its beliefs, values, assumptions, and attitudes.

The second aim of operational objectives is to evaluate efficiency. Assessment measures must be designed and monitored to be able to determine progress both quantitatively and qualitatively. An organization should aim to constantly learn by acquiring and interpreting data to improve progress, processes, products, and performance. These data and assessment points are critical not only for those involved in the organization's daily operations but also for the organization's leaders as they seek to develop appropriate accountability measures.

Operation—Initial Soil Assessment

1. Beyond strategic goals, do you have action steps that will lead you toward fulfilling your goals?
2. Are your plan's action steps guided by an expectation for short-term results (within one year or less)?
3. Does your plan include a means of feedback so that you will know when and how to improve?
4. Have you considered action steps that could change the organization's soil to promote future growth?
5. Does your plan include action steps for everyone in the organization? Engagement at each level will ensure greater buy-in.

7. *Implementation:* An organization's future is reached, not through strategic planning, but through strategic implementation.

There are many organizations that plan well, both strategically and operationally. However, there are few that implement their plans well. Too often, organizations develop a comprehensive plan only to have it printed in a brochure, placed on the shelf or coffee table, and then be forgotten.

In these instances, organizations resort to making decisions on an ad hoc basis and establish departmental power bases to compete for resources. At the same time, these organizations are struggling to survive among paths, rocks, or weeds.

Leaders cannot assume that the planning cycle is complete once the strategic goals are defined; the goals must be operationalized and implemented. Implementation is perhaps the most difficult step of moving an organization from deficient to rich soil. However, it is also the step that takes initiatives from ideas to reality.

The word "discipline" often has negative connotations, but in the organizational sense, discipline provides a practicable operational framework. Discipline provides consistency, enhances the company's ability to perform, and allows for effective teamwork. When implemented through policies, structure, and resource allocation, discipline allows individuals to flourish in their roles without micromanagement. Beyond this, organizational discipline also provides a structure to encourage creativity and problem solving.

The capstone of implementation is sustainability. Sustainability takes root when the organizational culture is shaped by an understanding that mission and vision fulfillment depends on the implementation of both strategic and operational plans. Over time, when fortified by implementation, the processes that produce a defined mission and vision, as well as strategic goals and operational objectives, coalesce into shared values and beliefs that, in turn, become key characteristics of the organization's identity.

Implementation—Initial Soil Assessment

1. Do you have periodic checkpoints to ensure that the organization makes progress toward its goals?
2. Do you set aside times for the community to recognize its progress?
3. Are you flexible enough to shift strategies once organizational plans are put into practice?
4. Is there sufficient organizational willpower and discipline to pursue goals in the face of resistance?
5. If the organization is not currently in rich soil, does a faulty implementation process account for the organization's more widespread deficiencies?

8. *Leadership:* The profession of leadership must be practiced.

Ultimately, the responsibility to move into rich soil belongs to the leadership. Among the most critical leadership qualities are determination, perseverance, and a desire to actually lead—that is, to do the dirty work of leadership regardless of whether you gain friends or accolades along the way.

Leading an organization is one of the most challenging professional roles that you can accept; leadership is typically not a comfortable role. A leader must be committed to embracing the demands of leadership, which may very well include personal sacrifices.

The practice of good leadership comes through a commitment to *pursue* leadership rather than simply *preside* in a leadership role. That is, a leader's heart and soul must be fully invested in the organization if it is to move into rich soil. Determining where the organization is, where it should be, and how to move toward the desired vision is the primary role of the leader. Thus the leader is ultimately responsible for the organizational soil.

A key role in leadership is to inspire team members and foster ownership. If a leader can't work through others, the organization's growth will be stunted. Working through others is accomplished, in part, by following the first few Rich Soil Elements. When leaders involve constituents in affirming the mission, creating a vision, and ensuring clarity, the organization flourishes.

Ultimately, a leader must continually cultivate the soil by inspiring teammates to accomplish more than they believed possible, even when growth doesn't seem to be occurring. Though it is challenging to tend the soil, the venture can succeed when a leader exhibits vision and drive and pursues a high standard of excellence.

Anyone seeking a leadership role must have a solid understanding of not just the role but of his or her own capabilities and motivations. A leader must truthfully answer three key questions before assuming a leadership role: Do you know yourself? Do you understand the expectations of your role? Are you being true to yourself?

First, do you know yourself? That is, do you understand your own gifts, abilities, limitations, and interests? Which critical leadership qualities do you exhibit? What motivates you?

Next, do you understand the expectations of your role? What type of leader does the organization need in its current stage of organizational development? What challenges does the organization face? Which type of soil is the organization currently functioning in, and what will be required to move it into rich soil?

Finally, you must ask yourself, do the answers to the previous questions align? Are you the right leader needed for this particular time and this particular organization? If they align, you should pursue the role. But if your answers do not align, or if they become misaligned over time, decline the role or remove yourself from it.

In all, you must be true to yourself. As tempting as it may be to believe you can overcome any misalignment by sheer willpower, be wary of making a poor decision that will result in failed leadership.

Leadership, in the fullest sense, then, is the thread that weaves together each step toward rich soil. Leadership provides the organization with the momentum it needs to continue developing and improving.

Not everyone is a leader. But every organization needs one. Discovering the right fit is the key.

Leadership—Initial Soil Assessment

1. Do you believe in the mission of the organization?
2. Are you more interested in presiding in a leadership role or pursuing a leadership role? (Those who preside are more satisfied with the status quo, while those who pursue constantly ask how performance can be improved.)
3. Do you understand your strengths as a leader and know how to build a team to compensate for your weaknesses?
4. Does the organization need the type of leadership you provide? Do you understand the expectations of the role, and can you meet them?

5. Do you believe the organization can achieve more in the future than it has in the past? Do you believe your leadership can make a difference in that regard?

Soil Assessment: Summary and Conclusion

Though soil that is improperly cared for has little value, even poor soil can be improved with proper care. The first steps toward improvement are identifying your organization's deficient soil and working to recultivate it. Then comes the more challenging task of nurturing the soil so that it remains fertile and productive. It is only when the soil is carefully maintained that organizational performance can flourish.

Every organization is different. What is required for an organization to improve will depend on the soil it is operating in, its vision, and its organizational culture. Thus the soil assessment is designed to accomplish two objectives: (1) identify the "type" of organizational soil, and (2) identify specific soil deficiencies according to the eight characteristics of rich soil.

Once again, reflect on your organization. What type of soil does it operate in? Is your soil an asset or liability? Does it provide the nutrients necessary for long-term growth and value?

This book has attempted to spark your thinking about how to maximize your organization's performance. Because a deficiency in any one area will result in the slowing or even the halting of organizational development, which can in turn decrease productivity and performance, each element in the framework is a critical component of your organization's success. Today's market is filled with aggressive competitors, strategic ruts, and bureaucratic roadblocks, but by applying the eight elements outlined above, you can take steps to live out your mission and vision and thrive in rich soil.

View leadership through the lens of grace.

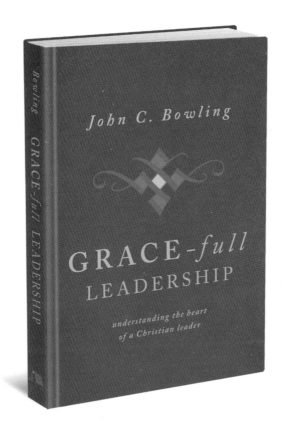

God has redefined the world of management for the Christian leader through Scripture. In *Grace-Full Leadership*, Bowling explores the leadership qualities and practices that are distinct within the community of Christian leadership. Discover how to become a leader who generates exponential growth in spiritual gains—an eternity of difference from today's capital gains.

Grace-Full Leadership
Understanding the Heart of a Christian Leader
By John C. Bowling
ISBN 978-0-8341-2602-2

www.BeaconHillBooks.com

BEACON HILL PRESS
OF KANSAS CITY